**Alfred's**
Teach Your Child To Play Guitar

Book 1

Ages 5 and Up

The Easiest Guitar Method Ever!

Nathaniel Gunod

L. C. Harnsberger

Ron Manus

Alfred

Alfred Music
P.O. Box 10003
Van Nuys, CA 91410-0003
alfred.com

D1378837

ISBN-10: 0-7390-9541-2
ISBN-13: 978-0-7390-9541-6

Cover and interior illustrations by Jeff Shelly.

 Contents printed on
environmentally responsible paper.

To the Parents

Guitar is one of the most commonly played instruments in the world. It is featured in both popular music and on the classical concert stage. It's portability makes it great for accompanying solo or group singing, so having a guitarist in the family can add a fun element to family gatherings of all kinds. Consequently, many parents want to share the joy of music making on the guitar with their children. They begin this process by teaching children the basics of guitar before getting them involved in formal guitar lessons with a professional teacher.

About This Book

This book is designed for any family wishing to get their young children started on the guitar, including those involved in homeschooling who wish to add it to the curriculum. It makes no assumptions of knowledge or skill on the part of the parent. Anyone, whether they have ever played music before or not, can use this book with their child. The step-by-step method provides lessons in the basics of music, while enabling students to start strumming chords to play along with fun children's songs right away. The accompanying audio demonstrates how the music sounds, and each lesson is explained in clear, plain language that is easy to understand.

A Parent Guide page precedes each student page. Most guide pages suggest steps for introducing the page to the student, follow-up practice ideas, and suggestions for reviewing the concepts and/or skills in subsequent lessons. To help with planning, space is often provided where parents can write notes pertaining to the lessons.

The CD contains a recording of every example in the book. It is fun for the student to listen or play along, but more importantly, it will reinforce musical concepts such as rhythm and dynamics. For convenience, you may download the audio onto an MP3 player or other digital music player, such as an iPod.

About the Lessons

Parents should set aside a regular lesson time each week for the child and strictly adhere to this schedule. It can be made a fun, pretend time for you both, where the student must knock to enter the lesson room and call the parent "Teacher." This will help make lesson time a special time, separate from normal family activities. Any parent can be very effective getting a child started on the guitar, but at some point the child will need the guidance of a professional guitarist/teacher. Another teacher should be sought when the materials are beyond the parent's understanding, or when lessons create tension in the household.

Page 96 contains some frequently asked questions about teaching a child. Enjoy sharing music and the guitar together!

Contents

Selecting Your Guitar

The guitar you choose for your child can make a significant impact on their success in learning to play. Starting out on a guitar that is too large can lead to frustration, slow progress, and even poor technique. Fortunately, guitars come in different sizes.

The Size of the Guitar—Accessibility

When holding the guitar properly, the child should be able to easily reach all six strings of the guitar with their right hand, and both the highest and lowest frets with their left, without changing the position of their shoulders or spine. Children aged 4–6 (3'3" to 3'9") are usually better off with a ¼ size guitar. Some parents even choose a baritone ukulele as a "first guitar," and that is fine for everything in this book. Children 5–8 years old (3'10" to 4'5") are often best-suited to a ½ size guitar, and a ¾ size guitar is usually the best choice for a child 8–11 years of age (4'6" to 4'11").

The Action

Another important issue is that some guitars are more difficult to play because the strings are set too high off the fretboard and are thus difficult to press down. The distance (gap) between the strings and the frets of the guitar is called the *action*. It is possible, of course, for the action to be set too low, causing unpleasant rattling noises on every note or strum. Either of these conditions—an action that is high or too low—would cause frustration for the student. When shopping for your guitar, be sure to ask the music store's guitar specialist about the action of the guitars you are considering. See if you can have your child try the Butterfly Finger Exercise on page 16. If it is too difficult and painful for the child to press down the string, the action may be set too high.

Steel Strings vs. Nylon Strings

Steel strings come on many acoustic guitars, and virtually all electric guitars. They come in a variety of *gauges*, or thicknesses. Guitar experts choose gauges that both feel and sound best to them. For a beginning guitar student, lighter-gauge strings are best, because they are easier to press down.

Nylon strings come on classical guitars, which are a type of acoustic guitar generally used for classical, flamenco, and some folk guitar music. Many experts prefer nylon strings for beginners, because they are easier on the fingers than steel strings. Some acoustic-electric guitars have nylon strings, too.

Selecting Your Guitar

Guitars come in different types and sizes. It's important to choose a guitar that's just the right size for you, and not one that's too big.

TOO BIG!

Just right.

Guitars come in three basic sizes: 1/2 size, 3/4 size, and full size. You should look and feel comfortable holding your guitar, so it's a good idea to have your local music store's guitar specialist evaluate if your guitar is the right size.

If the 1/2 size guitar is still too big for you, a baritone ukulele can be used instead of a guitar to learn everything up to page 74 of this course.

Baritone uke   1/2 size   3/4 size   Full size

Steel Strings and Nylon Strings

Steel strings are found on both acoustic and electric guitars. They have a bright and brassy sound.

Nylon strings are usually found on classical and flamenco guitars. They have a mellow, delicate sound. Nylon strings are often easier for beginners to play because they are easier on the fingers than steel strings.

Acoustic Guitars and Electric Guitars

Most young children will be happy with whatever type of guitar a parent provides. Sometimes, though, a child is motivated to learn guitar through their admiration for a specific artist and thus want a specific type of guitar—they want to be "just like" their guitar idol. When possible, it is a good idea to allow the student to use the guitar of their choice, so they will be motivated to pick it up and practice playing every day.

It is important to note that choosing an electric guitar will lead to the purchase of an amplifier and cable, too. Both the electric guitar and the amplifier have volume controls, so there's no need for the playing to become too loud. Many amplifiers come with built in distortion and other effects. For the sake of a good lesson and productive practice, these effects should not be used. They can be part of non-practice, "just-for-fun" guitar time.

Introducing the Parts of the Guitar

For a very young child, it can be fun to make up a name for the guitar, and introduce it to your child as a new friend with three main parts—a head, neck, and body—just like a person!

1. While you carefully hold your child's guitar, oriented vertically, with the strap peg lightly resting on the floor (a soft rug is recommended) and the headstock in one hand, introduce the headstock, neck, and body by pointing with the other hand while you say the name.

2. Now, play a game where you point to the part, and your child says its name. Make the pointing-and-naming game fun! Perhaps choose some appropriate prizes for correct answers.

Practice Suggestions

1. At every lesson or practice session, introduce one or two new parts.

2. Play the pointing-and-naming game including all the parts that have been covered in your sessions.

Subsequent Lessons

Continue to add new parts to the game at every session until your child knows the names of the parts so well, the game loses its luster. It's a good idea, however, to bring the game back every once in a while, just to make sure your child remembers the parts. It can be a good way to break up a serious lesson and make it more fun.

Acoustic Guitars and Electric Guitars

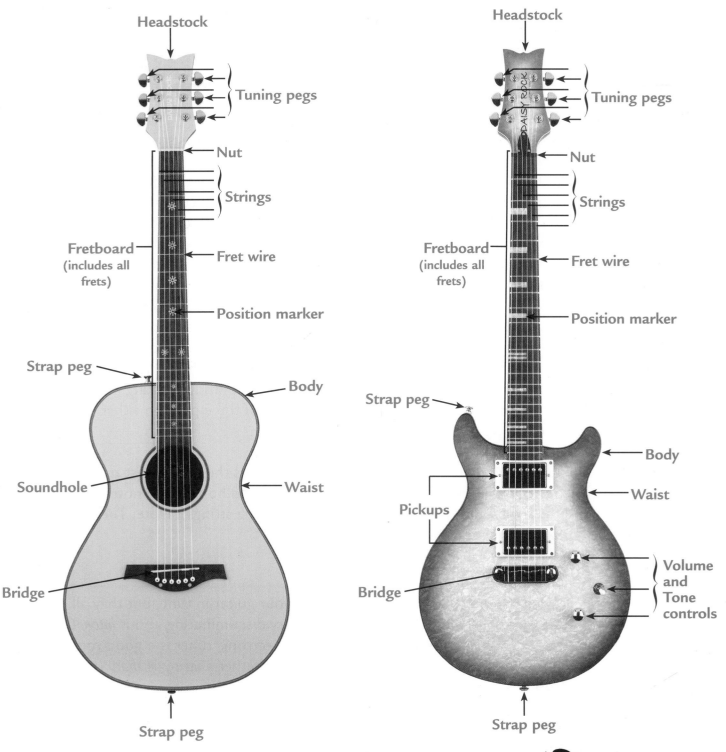

Headstock

Tuning pegs

Nut

Strings

Fretboard (includes all frets)

Fret wire

Position marker

Strap peg

Body

Soundhole

Waist

Bridge

Strap peg

Headstock

Tuning pegs

Nut

Strings

Fretboard (includes all frets)

Fret wire

Position marker

Strap peg

Body

Pickups

Waist

Bridge

Volume and Tone controls

Strap peg

Caring for Your Guitar

Get to know your guitar and treat it like a friend. When you carry it, think of it as part of your body so you don't accidentally bump it against walls or furniture, and be especially sure not to drop it! Every time you're done playing, carefully dust off your guitar with a soft cloth, and be sure to put it away in its case.

Tuning Your Guitar

Your child's music making will be most successful when the guitar is in tune. While it is possible for a guitar to be just "in tune with itself," it is best to be in tune with a standard pitch from either an in-tune piano, a tuning fork, a pitch pipe, or the CD that comes with this book. You can also use an electronic tuner or a tuning app for your mobil device that "listens" to each string and tells you whether or not it is in tune. With the guitar tuned properly, your family sing-alongs can include the guitar along with other properly tuned instruments.

Stringing the Guitar

Strings do not last forever. A professional guitarist changes strings fairly often, so their guitar always sounds its best. Old strings can sound dull and lifeless, and eventually become difficult to tune. Until your child is old enough to string the instrument, it will be up to you to make sure it is strung correctly before getting it in tune. Either take the instrument to a local music store or pick up a book like *I Just Bought My First Guitar* (22705) that will lead you step-by-step.

There are different styles of headstock and tuning pegs, but your guitar will be strung when you buy it, so observe how it is done and even take a photograph. That way, when it is time to replace a broken string (it happens), or put on a whole new set, you'll have a model to follow. Strings should go from the inside to the outside, so that turning the peg counterclockwise tightens it, making it sound higher. Turning the peg clockwise should loosen the string, making it sound lower. The directions are reversed when there is a row of three pegs on either side of the headstock.

On a standard guitar, the thinnest, highest string is the one closest to the floor when the guitar is held normally (with the left hand holding the notes on the neck, and the right hand strumming and/or plucking the strings). Note: There are also left-handed guitars, which are strung in reverse*.

Getting in Tune

Following the directions on page 9 will get your guitar in tune, but they all require careful listening. One learns to be very discriminating about *intonation* (the accuracy of the tuning) with experience. An electronic tuner is a good tool for learning good intonation, as it will show you whether a string is *sharp* (too high) or *flat* (too low), and by how much.

Be very careful when tuning a string up or tightening it. Tuning a string too high can cause it to break. Always listen as you slowly turn the peg, bit-by-bit. That way, you'll hear if you are turning the peg too rapidly and tuning the string too high. In other words: never turn a tuning peg without plucking the string and listening.

* It is not necessary for a left-handed student to have a left-handed guitar. That is a personal choice. The authors believe there is no real advantage to left-handed guitars for left-handed players. Should you choose a left-handed guitar for your child, simply reverse the directional instructions in this book.

Tuning Your Guitar

First make sure your strings are wound properly around the tuning pegs. They should go from the inside to the outside, as in the picture. Some guitars have all six tuning pegs on the same side of the headstock, and in this case make sure all six strings are wound the same way, from inside out.

Turning a tuning peg clockwise makes the pitch lower. Turning a tuning peg counter-clockwise makes the pitch higher. Be sure not to tune the strings too high because they could break!

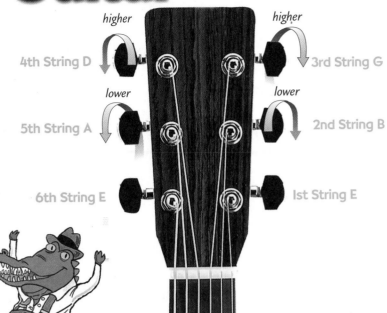

higher
4th String D
lower
5th String A
6th String E

higher
3rd String G
lower
2nd String B
1st String E

Important:

Always remember that the thinnest, highest-sounding string, the one closest to the floor, is the first string. The thickest, lowest-sounding string, the one closest to the ceiling, is the sixth string. When guitarists say "the highest string," they mean the highest-sounding string.

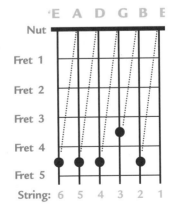

Ceiling

Lowest String

Floor

Highest String

Tuning with the CD

 Tracks 1 & 2

Using Your CD Player
Put the CD in your CD player and play Tracks 1 and 2. Listen to the directions and match each of your guitar's strings to its pitch on the CD.

Tuning without the CD

Tuning the Guitar to Itself
When your sixth string is in tune, you can tune the rest of the strings just using the guitar alone. First, tune the sixth string to E on the piano, then follow the instructions to the right to get the guitar in tune.

Press 5th fret of 6th string to get pitch of 5th string (A).

Press 5th fret of 5th string to get pitch of 4th string (D).

Press 5th fret of 4th string to get pitch of 3rd string (G).

Press 4th fret of 3rd string to get pitch of 2nd string (B).

Press 5th fret of 2nd string to get pitch of 1st string (E).

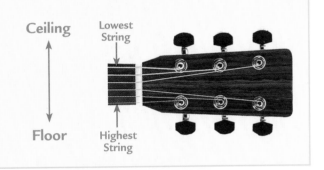

E A D G B E
Nut
Fret 1
Fret 2
Fret 3
Fret 4
Fret 5
String: 6 5 4 3 2 1

Pitch Pipes and Electronic Tuners
If you don't have a piano available, buying an electronic tuner or pitch pipe is recommended. The salesperson at your music store can show you how to use them.

How to Hold Your Guitar

The position of the student's body and the position of the guitar relative to the student's body are the foundations of his or her guitar technique. With the body and hands positioned optimally, learning the guitar is easiest. Your child should always have good posture when playing the guitar and be aware of the guitar's position.

Introducing the Concept

While there is not one correct way for your child to hold the guitar (page 11 shows just a few of the available options), there are some common-sense guidelines to keep in mind for the best results:

1. The student's spine should be straight. Avoid leaning to the right or left, or "hunching over" the instrument.

2. The shoulders should be level. Avoid elevating either shoulder, or thrusting it forward or backward.

3. The left hand should be able to comfortably reach every fret, from the lowest to the highest, without changing the position of the spine or either shoulder.

4. The right arm should be able to move freely from the elbow, up and down, without feeling limited by the outer edge of the guitar body or moving the right shoulder.

Practice Suggestions

1. Check the four points above every time your child gets ready to play.

2. Recheck their posture before each example or song.

Subsequent Lessons

Don't worry if you have to work on posture and position at every lesson. This will be an ongoing process and will require attention for quite some time.

Notes:

How to Hold Your Guitar

Hold your guitar in the position that
is most comfortable for you.
Some positions are shown below.

Sitting

Sitting with legs crossed

Standing with strap

When you practice on your
own or want to play just for
fun, you might feel comfortable
sitting cross-legged on the floor
or on your bed. Just be sure to
keep good posture with your
back straight.

Sitting on the floor

Strumming the Strings

Now that your child is holding the guitar properly, it is time to begin playing. Strumming will be a fun and exciting activity. The idea is to brush quickly across all six strings, causing them all to sound together.

Strumming with a Pick

A guitar *pick*, or *plectrum*, is generally made of one uniform material, such as plastic or nylon. They are usually triangle shaped, with two of the corners very rounded and one slightly less rounded. The less-rounded corner is typically the part used to strike the strings.

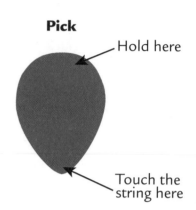

Pick

Hold here

Touch the string here

Introducing the Pick

1. Help your child get into a good position with their guitar, ready to play.
2. Show them the pick and point out the less-rounded corner, explaining that it is the strumming end. Demonstrate strumming with the pick.
3. Have your child hold their right arm out in front of them, keeping the forearm in contact with the body of the guitar.
4. Have them hold their fingers in a comfortably curled position, like holding a ball.
5. Place the pick on the tip joint of the finger, with the less-rounded corner pointed out, away from the palm of the hand.
6. Have your child place their thumb on the pick and hold it firmly. Make sure they don't squeeze the pick too hard...they should just hold it firmly in place.
7. Help the student place the tip of the pick on the lowest, 6th string, and, moving from the wrist with a little help from the elbow joint, move it quickly and firmly across all six strings to create a strum.

Strumming with the Fingers

Some students prefer to strum with their fingers. Two popular ways to do this are: 1) with the thumb, or 2) with the back of the nail of the index finger. Either way is fine. Demonstrate both methods and have your child try both. Refer to the pictures on page 13.

Practice Suggestions

1. Tap a slow, steady beat on your lap, and count aloud, saying "1 2 3 4 5 6 7 8."
2. Using their chosen strumming method, have them strum the strings while counting aloud.
3. Play along with Track 3 on the CD.

Subsequent Lessons

1. If using a pick, remind the student to hold it firmly but not to squeeze too hard. The idea is to make a solid, firm sound.
2. Always encourage your child to keep a slow, steady beat as they strum.

Strumming the Strings

To *strum* means to play the strings with your right hand by brushing quickly across them. There are two common ways of strumming the strings. One is with your fingers, and the other is with a pick.

Strumming with a Pick

Hold the pick between your thumb and index finger. Hold it firmly, but don't squeeze it too hard.

Strum from the sixth string (the thickest, lowest-sounding string) to the first string (the thinnest, highest-sounding string).

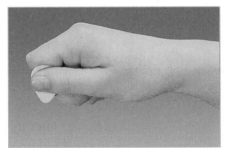

Start near the top string.

Move mostly your wrist, not just your arm. Finish near the bottom string.

Strumming with Your Fingers

First decide if you feel more comfortable strumming with the side of your thumb or the nail of your index finger. The strumming motion is the same with the thumb or finger as it is when using the pick. Strum from the sixth string (the thickest, lowest-sounding string) to the first string (the thinnest, highest-sounding string).

Strumming with the thumb

Strumming with the index finger

> ## Important:
> Strum by mostly moving your wrist, not just your arm. Use as little motion as possible. Start as close to the top string as you can, and never let your hand move past the edge of the guitar.

Time to Strum! Track 3

Strum all six strings slowly and evenly.

Count your strums out loud as you play.

Repeat this exercise until you feel comfortable strumming the strings.

	strum	strum	strum	strum	strum	strum	strum	strum
	/	/	/	/	/	/	/	/
Count:	1	2	3	4	5	6	7	8

Strumming Notation

Guitar strums are often written with slash-style notation. Most notational styles indicate how long each musical sound lasts. We measure musical time with *beats*, which are the steady pulse of the music. The *rhythm* is the pattern of note durations against the beat. A *quarter-note* strum is written with a slash and a stem, as shown on page 15. A quarter-note slash gets one beat.

Introducing the Page

Discuss beats with the student. Relating beats to the steady tick-tock of a clock is helpful. Introduce the *staff* as a picture of the time in which the music will happen, and the *bar lines* as a way to divide the time into groups of beats, called *measures*. The *time signature*, which always appears at the beginning, is there to tell us how many beats go in each measure.

Practice Suggestions

1. Point to the quarter-note slashes in "More Time to Strum" and count aloud, slowly and evenly, saying "1 2 3 4 1 2 3 4."

2. Strum across the strings while counting aloud.

3. Try strumming just the highest three strings (the three strings closest to the floor), strings 3, 2, and 1. Do this several times, until it is easy.

4. Now, counting aloud slowly and evenly, play "More Time to Strum" on just the top three strings.

Subsequent Lessons

1. Make it part of the routine to point at the notes of a song or example while slowly and evenly counting aloud.

2. Play along with Track 4 of the CD.

Notes:

Strumming Notation

Beats

Each strum you play is equal to one *beat*. Beats are even, like the ticking of a clock.

tick - tick - tick - tick
beat-beat-beat-beat

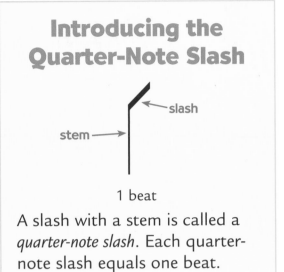
The Staff and Treble Clef

Guitar music is usually written on a five-line *staff* that has a *treble clef* at its beginning.

Treble clef

5
4
3
2
1

Bar Lines, Measures, and Time Signatures

Bar lines divide the staff into equal parts called measures. A *double bar line* is used at the end to show you the music is finished.

Measures are always filled with a certain number of beats. You know how many beats are in each measure by looking at the *time signature*, which is always at the beginning of the music. A $\frac{4}{4}$ time signature ("four-four time") means there are 4 equal beats in every measure.

Bar lines

Double bar line

measure   measure

Time signature

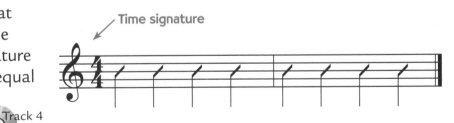

More Time to Strum

Track 4

Play this example in $\frac{4}{4}$ time. It will sound the same as "Time to Strum," which you played on the previous page. Keep the beats even and count out loud.

First time: Strum all six strings as you did before.

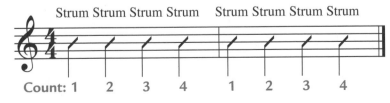

Strum Strum Strum Strum   Strum Strum Strum Strum

Count: 1   2   3   4   1   2   3   4

Strumming strings 3–2–1

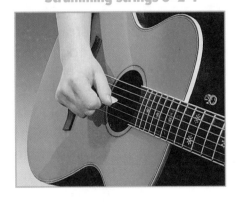

Second time: Strum starting with the third string, and strum only strings 3, 2, and 1.

15

Using Your Left Hand

The job of a left-hand finger is to shorten the vibrating string length by pressing the string into a fret. The shorter the vibrating string, the higher the *pitch* (pitch is the highness or lowness of the sound). Note that we *do not press the string into the wood of the fretboard.* It is by pressing the string securely into the fret wire that we change the vibrating length of the string, so the most efficient left-hand technique is one that accomplishes this using as little strength as necessary. Be sure to review How to Read Chord Diagrams with your child.

Introducing the Left-Hand Fingers

Numbers are given to the left-hand fingers for easy identification. The fingers are numbered consecutively, with the index finger being 1 and the pinky, 4.

1. Have your child hold up their left hand. Point to each finger and say the corresponding finger number.

2. Repeat, but this time, ask your child to say the finger number as you point.

Practice Suggestions

1. Have your child trace their left hand on a separate piece of paper. Then, number each finger.

2. Have your child hold up their left hand. As you call out finger numbers, have them wiggle the correct finger.

Hand Position and Placing a Finger on a String

Fingers are naturally stronger and will provide the best leverage in a curled position, like gently holding a ball. The left thumb should be in the middle of the back of the guitar neck, between fingers 1 and 2. Keeping the elbow loosely in and the fingers curled, use the very tips of the fingers to press the strings, placing them directly next to the fret wire, but not actually ON the fret.

Practice Suggestion—Butterfly Finger Exercise

1. Using the photos on page 17 as a guide, have your child lightly place finger 1 , without pressing down, on the 2nd string, right next to the 1st fret. You can say the finger should be "like a butterfly landing on the string."

2. Ask him or her to pluck the 2nd string with the pick or right-hand finger. You will hear a clicking, unpitched sound. No note will be heard.

3. Have your child slowly begin to add pressure with the finger as they pluck the string. The instant the string sings out a clear note, the student should stop adding pressure. That is as hard as he or she needs to press to play.

Subsequent Lessons

Your child may experience a little discomfort at first. It takes a while to develop calluses at the tips of the left-hand fingers. Keep practice sessions short to minimize associating discomfort with playing guitar, and always remind him or her that their fingers should not press hard or squeeze the neck. Repeat the "butterfly finger" exercise described above often.

Using Your Left Hand

Hand Position

Learning to use your left-hand fingers easily starts with a good hand position. Place your hand so your thumb rests comfortably in the middle of the back of the neck. Position your fingers on the front of the neck as if you are gently squeezing a ball between them and your thumb. Keep your elbow in and your fingers curved.

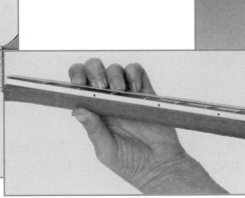

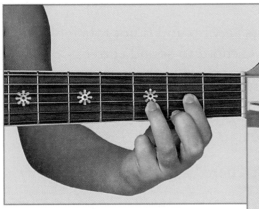

Keep elbow in and fingers curved

Like gently squeezing a ball between your fingertips and thumb

Placing a Finger on a String

When you press a string with a left-hand finger, make sure you press firmly with the tip of your finger and as close to the fret wire as you can without actually being right on it. Short fingernails are important! This will create a clean, bright tone.

RIGHT
Finger presses the string down near the fret without actually being on it.

WRONG
Finger is too far from fret wire; tone is "buzzy" and indefinite.

WRONG
Finger is on top of fret wire; tone is muffled and unclear.

How to Read Chord Diagrams

Chord diagrams show where to place your fingers. The example to the right shows finger 1 on the first string at the first fret. The Xs above the sixth, fifth and fourth strings tell you not to play them and only strum the third, second and first strings. Strings that are not played in a chord also look like dashed lines. The os above the second and third strings tell you these strings are to be played *open*, meaning without pressing down on them with a left-hand finger.

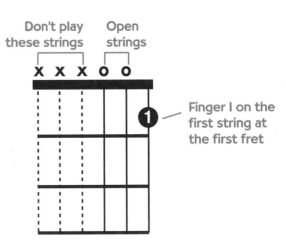

Don't play these strings   Open strings

Finger I on the first string at the first fret

The Three-String C Chord

Combined with holding the guitar properly and a good left-hand position, properly curled fingers will make playing a C chord fun and easy for your child.

Introducing the C Chord

1. Practice strumming the top three strings using "More Time to Strum" on page 15.

2. Repeat the Butterfly Finger Exercise from page 16.

3. Together, listen to the audio for Track 5.

4. Make sure finger 1 is up on the left side of its very tip and is not touching the 1st string, which needs to ring freely for the C chord to sound correct.

5. While holding down the 2nd string at the 1st fret, strum the top three strings.

Practice Suggestions

1. Point at each quarter-note slash in "My First Chord" as you slowly and evenly count aloud, saying "1 2 3 4 1 2 3 4."

2. Counting aloud, slowly strum "My First Chord."

3. When strumming this song feels comfortable and easy, try playing along with the audio for Track 6.

Subsequent Lessons

Continue to remind your child not to squeeze too hard with the 1st finger. Repeat the Butterfly Finger Exercise on page 16 often. It may take a little trial and error for your child to learn how to avoid bumping into the 1st string with the 1st finger when playing the C chord. Be patient and allow them to experiment with the finger position, remaining sensitive to potential discomfort. Keep practice sessions short.

Notes:

The Three-String C Chord

 **Hear this chord!** Track 5

Use finger 1 to press the 2nd string at the 1st fret.
Strum strings 3–2–1.

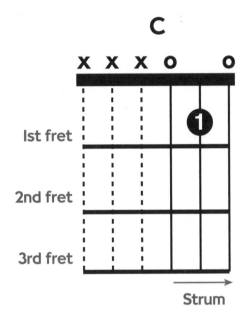

C

x x x o   o

1st fret

2nd fret

3rd fret

Strum

Strumming

Strum the three-string C chord on each quarter-note slash ⸍. Make sure your strums are even. Count aloud as you play:

1-2-3-4 | 1-2-3-4.

Listen to the song on your CD to hear how it should sound!

My First Chord Track 6

Remember: This means there are beats in each measure.

C
xxxo o

Count: 1   2   3   4   1   2   3   4
Strum Strum Strum the   Three - String C   Chord!

This **double bar line** tells us the music is finished.

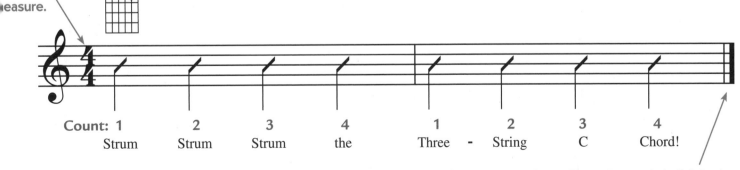

19

The Quarter Rest

Silence is a very important part of music, and it is indicated with a *rest* symbol. For every note value (such as a quarter note), there is an equal rest duration.

Introducing the Concept

Some say the quarter rest, which means one beat of silence, looks like a bird flying sideways, or a squiggly line. What does it look like to your child? That could be a fun conversation. Discuss the importance of silence in music, and how boring music would be if it never stopped.

1. Try singing "Three Blind Mice" without any silences or pauses. Wouldn't that be silly?

2. Show your child the rest position using the picture on top of page 21 as a reference.

3. Have your child place the pinky-side of their right hand across the strings, just to the left of the bridge. Introduce this as the *rest position*.

4. Now, have your child strum all of the strings, then place his or her hand in rest position to stop them from ringing.

5. Finally, practice the "Rest Warm-up" while slowly and evenly counting aloud, saying "1 2 3 rest 1 2 3 rest," assuming rest position every time you say "rest."

Practice Suggestions

1. Saying "1 2 3 rest 1 2 3 rest," etc., count aloud and point at each note and rest in "Three Blind Mice."

2. Position the left-hand 1st finger on the C chord, making sure all three strings are ringing clearly by plucking each of them separately.

3. Counting aloud, strum "Three Blind Mice," carefully performing all of the rests using the rest position.

4. Strum through "Three Blind Mice" while a friend or parent sings the words.

5. Play and sing the words yourself.

Subsequent Lessons

1. Continue practicing "Three Blind Mice" as needed.

2. Repeat the Butterfly Finger Exercise often.

3. Keep checking to make sure all three strings of the C chord are ringing clearly.

The Quarter Rest

Introducing the Quarter Rest

This strange-looking music symbol means to be silent for one beat. Stop the sound of the strings by lightly touching them with the side of your hand, as in the photo.

1 beat

Track 7

Rest Warm-up

Before playing "Three Blind Mice," practice this exercise until you are comfortable playing rests.

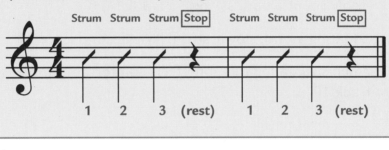

Strum Strum Strum Stop   Strum Strum Strum Stop

1   2   3   (rest)   1   2   3   (rest)

Practice Tip

Strum the chords and have a friend sing the words.

Three Blind Mice

Track 8   C

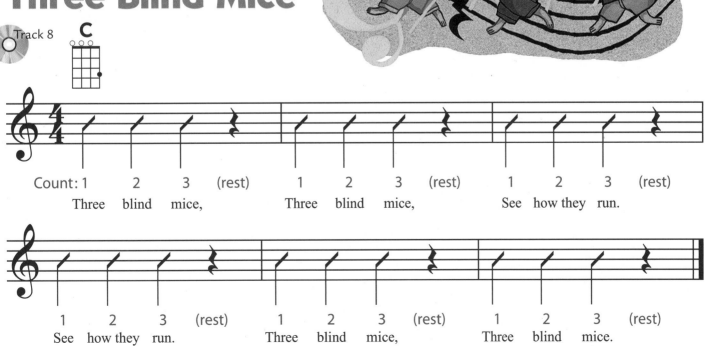

Count: 1   2   3   (rest)   1   2   3   (rest)   1   2   3   (rest)
Three blind mice,   Three blind mice,   See how they run.

1   2   3   (rest)   1   2   3   (rest)   1   2   3   (rest)
See how they run.   Three blind mice,   Three blind mice.

The Three-String G⁷ Chord

All "7" chords have a bluesy quality. This one is very easy and is a lot like the C chord. Just move the 1st finger to the 1st string.

Introducing the G⁷ Chord

1. Have your child position the left hand for the C chord, with the 1st finger on the 2nd string at the 1st fret.

2. Now, have them simply move the 1st finger over to the 1st string. Remember, we usually play a little to the left side of the tip of finger 1.

3. Together, listen to the audio for Track 9.

Practice Suggestions

1. Point at each quarter-note slash in "My Second Chord" as you slowly and evenly count aloud, saying "1 2 3 4 1 2 3 4."

2. Counting aloud, slowly strum "My Second Chord."

3. When strumming this song feels comfortable and easy, try playing along with Track 10.

Subsequent Lessons

Continue to remind your child not to squeeze too hard with the 1st finger. Repeat the Butterfly Finger Exercise on page 16 often. Remain sensitive to potential discomfort, and keep practice sessions short.

Notes:

The Three-String G⁷ Chord

Use finger 1 to press the 1st string at the 1st fret.
Strum strings 3–2–1.

G⁷

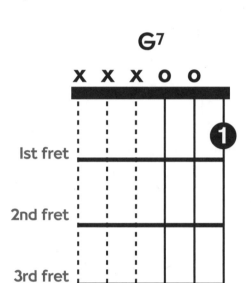

My Second Chord

Track 10

G⁷

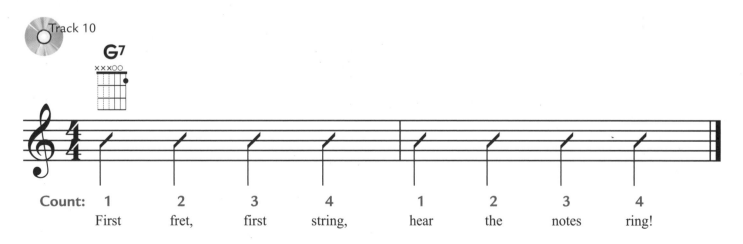

Count: 1   2   3   4   1   2   3   4
First fret, first string, hear the notes ring!

Troubadour Song

This song combines quarter rests with the two chords covered so far. Now is a good time to start singing "Skip to My Lou" around the house. It will be part of your guitar time, soon!

Introducing the Page

Follow these steps with your child:

1. Point at each note, naming the chord to play or saying "rest" (e.g., "C C C rest G^7 G^7 G^7 rest," etc.).

2. Now, ask your child to do this on their own.

3. Have your child, without strumming, switch the left-hand 1st finger from C to G^7, over and over, until it is easy to do.

Practice Suggestions

1. Play the right hand alone while counting aloud, saying "1 2 3 rest 1 2 3 rest," etc., being careful to use the rest position to perform the quarter rests. Use the rest as time to move the left hand and switch chords when there is a chord change.

2. Add the left hand, continuing to count aloud.

3. Try playing along with Track 11.

Subsequent Lessons

To your child, remembering to switch chords while performing the rests may feel, at first, a little like patting their head while rubbing their belly—it requires coordination that will have to be practiced. This is one of the many reasons learning an instrument is so wonderful for a young child. Gaining this sort of coordination does a lot for his or her mental development. It is worth the effort!

Notes:

Troubadour Song

Remember to stop the sound by lightly touching the strings with the side of your hand on each ≱. Wait one beat.

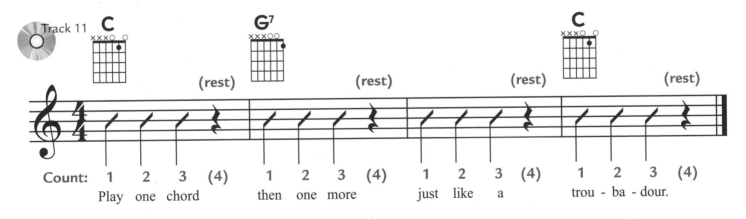

Track 11

C   G⁷   C

(rest)   (rest)   (rest)   (rest)

Count: 1 2 3 (4)   1 2 3 (4)   1 2 3 (4)   1 2 3 (4)
        Play one chord   then one more   just like a   trou - ba - dour.

*A troubadour was a musician who traveled around singing and playing.

25

Skip to My Lou

It's time to strum along with this classic children's song on the guitar! "Skip to My Lou" will provide further reinforcement of your child's guitar skills and knowledge. This time, though, there is no rest between the G^7 and C chords, which takes us to the next level. In the meantime, now is a good time to start singing "London Bridge" around the house (it's the next lesson!). Try it in the car, next time you drive over a bridge!

Introducing the Page

1. Review the music with your child, pointing out the last two measures and the chord change without a rest between the chords.

2. Without strumming, practice moving finger 1 from the 1st fret of the 2nd string to the 1st string, right next door, as described in the Practice Tip.

Practice Suggestions

1. Slowly and evenly point at each quarter-note slash and say the name of the chord, saying "rest" at the quarter rests.

2. Repeat this activity with your child.

3. As you slowly and evenly point at the quarter-note slashes and rests, say the lyrics to the song, demonstrating how the words fall against the beats.

4. Repeat this activity with your child.

5. As you tap the beats on your lap, say the lyrics to the song in rhythm as your child practices the left hand without strumming.

6. Repeat this activity, but have your child add in the strumming. They must be careful to strum only the top three strings.

Subsequent Lessons

Think about how many skills your child is combining to strum "Skip to My Lou": strumming in time, playing just the top three strings, using the rest position to perform the quarter rests, keeping finger 1 clear of the 1st string to play a C chord, changing directly from a G^7 chord to a C chord without a rest in between, and maintaining a good position with the hands and guitar, all at the same time!

That is a lot to coordinate! Plus, he or she may still be experiencing some discomfort when pressing down the strings with the 1st finger. Be patient and encouraging! This may take awhile to master. As you move onto the next lessons, return to "Skip to My Lou" and try playing along with Track 12, to keep things fun and interesting.

Skip to My Lou

G⁷   C

Practice Tip

To change quickly from G⁷ to C in the last two measures, just move your finger from the 1st string to the 2nd string—that's not very far.

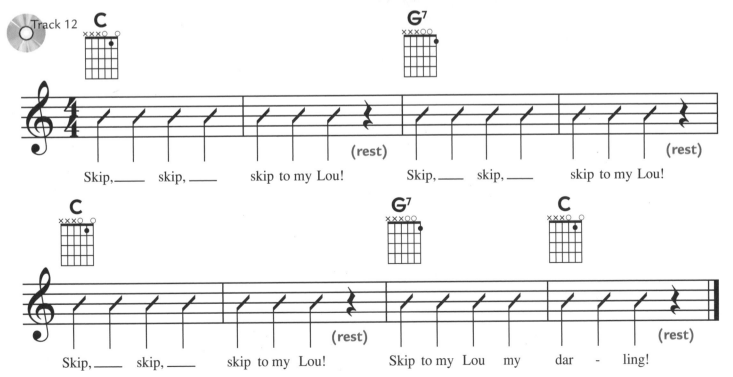

Track 12

Skip,—— skip, —— skip to my Lou!   Skip,—— skip, —— skip to my Lou!

Skip,—— skip, —— skip to my Lou!   Skip to my Lou my dar - ling!

27

London Bridge

Your child gets some more mileage out of all the skills they have learned with this fun song. There aren't any brand new skills, here, so just enjoy adding another children's classic to your repertoire.

Introducing the Page

1. Review the music with your child, pointing out the last two measures and the chord change without a rest between the chords.

2. Point out that the second line of music does not have a new chord frame at the beginning of the staff, so the C chord from the first line just continues.

Practice Suggestions

1. Slowly and evenly point at each quarter-note slash and say the name of the chord, saying "rest" at the quarter rests.

2. Repeat this activity with your child.

3. As you slowly and evenly point at the quarter-note slashes and rests, say the lyrics to the song, demonstrating how the words fall against the beats.

4. Repeat this activity with your child.

5. As you tap the beats on your lap, say the lyrics to the song in rhythm as your child practices the left hand without strumming.

6. Repeat this activity, but have your child add in the strumming. They must be careful to strum only the top three strings.

Subsequent Lessons

Think about how many skills your child is combining to strum "London Bridge": strumming in time, playing just the top three strings, keeping finger 1 clear of the 1st string to play a C chord, changing directly from a G^7 chord to a C chord without a rest in between, and maintaining a good position with the hands and guitar—all in one tune!

Notes:

London Bridge

Track 13

C

G⁷

C

Lon - don Bridge is   fal - ling down,   (rest)   fal - ling down,   (rest)   fal - ling   down   (rest)

(No new chord symbol, so keep playing C!)

G⁷

C

Lon - don Bridge is   fal - ling down,   (rest)   my____ fair____   la - dy.   (rest)

Remember to move first finger
quickly back to the 2nd string to
play the C chord on the next beat.

29

The Three-String G Chord

This chord is very easy. Just put finger 3 on the 1st string at the 3rd fret. By now, your child's 1st finger may be starting to develop calluses. It's time to "break in" another finger!

Introducing the G Chord

1. Have your child make an "okay" sign with his or her left thumb and finger 3. This will get the finger into a nicely curled position, very much like the finger position for playing the three-string G chord.

2. Now, have them make that "okay" sign with the 3rd fret of the 1st string between the thumb and 3rd finger.

3. Together, listen to Track 14.

Practice Suggestions

1. Point at each quarter-note slash in "My Third Chord" as you slowly and evenly count aloud, saying "1 2 3 4 1 2 3 4."

2. Counting aloud, slowly strum "My Third Chord."

3. When strumming this song is secure and easy, try playing along with Track 15.

Subsequent Lessons

Remind your child not to squeeze too hard with the 3rd finger. Repeat the Butterfly Finger Exercise on page 16, this time using the 3rd finger. Remain sensitive to potential discomfort, and keep practice sessions short.

Notes:

The Three-String G Chord

Use finger 3 to press the 1st string at the 3rd fret.
Strum strings 3–2–1.

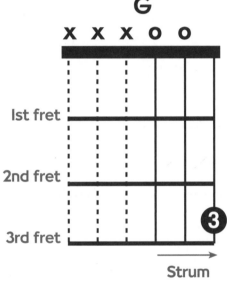

My Third Chord

Track 15

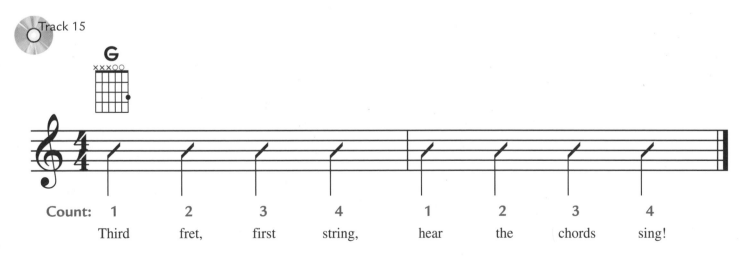

Count: 1   2   3   4   1   2   3   4
         Third   fret,   first   string,   hear   the   chords   sing!

Three Chords in One Song

This song combines all three chords we've covered, plus rests. By now, your child should be developing some good practice habits, so putting three chords all together to play a song should be an attainable goal. This is a good time to start singing "Merrily We Roll Along" and "Love Somebody" around the house—two classic folk songs. Have fun!

Introducing the Page

Together, begin by slowly playing each of the three chords—C, G^7, and G—and discuss the different finger positions used to play them.

1. Since we must stay clear of the adjacent string to play a C chord, finger 1 needs to stand up nice and straight on the left side of the tip of the finger.

2. For the G^7 chord, finger 1 is probably not standing up quite as straight, but we are still on the left side of the very tip of the finger. It's similar to the finger position for the C chord.

3. For the G chord, we are right up on the center of the tip of finger 3, making an "okay" sign.

4. Now, discuss the content of the "Remember" box on page 33—you'll have to take things slowly since "Rain Comes Down" features three chords, quarter rests, and chords that change in almost every measure.

5. Can your child find the ONE measure in "Rain Comes Down" that does NOT have a chord change?

6. Ask your child to find the ONE measure in "Rain Comes Down" that does NOT have a quarter rest.

Practice Suggestions

1. Point at each quarter-note slash and rest in "Rain Comes Down" as you slowly and evenly count aloud, saying "1 2 3 rest 1 2 3 rest." Take special note of the one measure where there is no rest.

2. Practice going from measure 1 into measure 2 several times—C to G is a new chord change.

3. Use the rests as an opportunity to move a finger to the next chord.

4. Counting aloud, slowly strum "Rain Comes Down."

5. When strumming this song is comfortable and easy, try playing along with Track 16.

Subsequent Lessons

Remember to stay vigilant about your child's playing position. Are their shoulders level and relaxed? Is their spine straight? Is their left arm hanging loosely in and not poking out to the left? Keep your child's foundation solid!

Three Chords in One Song

C

G⁷

G

Remember:
This song has three different chords in it. At first, take your time and play slowly so that all the notes sound clearly. Don't forget to be silent for a beat on each quarter rest as you change to a new chord.

Rain Comes Down

Track 16

| C | G | G⁷ | C |

Count: 1   2   3   (rest)   1   2   3   (rest)   1   2   3   (rest)   1   2   3   4
Tap   tap   tap,   rain comes down,   from   the sky   to   the ground.___

| G | G⁷ | C |

1   2   3   (rest)   1   2   3   (rest)   1   2   3   (rest)   1   2   3   (rest)
Tap   tap   tap,   hear   the   beat.   Rain - drops fall   all   a - round.

33

The Repeat Sign

The left-facing *repeat sign* simply tells us to go back to the beginning and play again. In this case, when we perform "Merrily We Roll Along," we get to play it twice!

Introducing the Page

Show your child the repeat sign, and explain that it means to go back to the beginning and play again *without any break in the counting*. This is a good opportunity to mention that musicians try to look ahead in the music as they play. Also, explain how the quarter rest on the last beat of measure 8 can be used to move his or her eyes to the beginning of the song and be ready to continue.

Practice Suggestions

1. Point at each quarter-note slash and quarter rest in "Merrily We Roll Along" as you slowly and evenly count aloud, saying "1 2 3 4 1 2 3 rest," etc. When you come to the repeat, it's very important to keep the beat absolutely steady as you go from pointing at the quarter rest on the last beat to pointing at the quarter-note slash on the first beat.

2. Now, do this activity together with your child.

3. Practice playing measures 7 and 8 into measure 1 several times, focusing on keeping a steady beat.

4. Once that feels comfortable, play the whole song and have fun!

Subsequent Lessons

Remind your child not to squeeze the notes too hard. Here's a fun trick to try.

1. Cut a small piece of paper off of a larger sheet. Your piece should be about two inches long and half an inch wide.

2. Have your child put his or her 3rd finger down on the 1st string at the 3rd fret, to play a G chord.

3. Do the Butterfly Finger Exercise from page 16.

4. Now, while your child keeps the 3rd finger on its note, freely strumming the G chord, slip your piece of paper under the string. Yes! You should be able to move the paper freely under the finger without affecting the sound of the chord! The string should *not* be touching the wood of the fretboard!

5. Together, play along with Track 17.

Notes:

The Repeat Sign

Introducing the Repeat Sign :‖

Double dots on the inside of a double bar line mean to go back to the beginning and play again.

Merrily We Roll Along

Track 17

C   G   C

Mer - ri - ly we roll a - long, roll a - long, roll a - long.

G⁷   C

Mer - ri - ly we roll a - long ____ o'er the deep blue sea. _____

Repeat from the beginning

Love Somebody

Learning to play "Love Somebody" is another opportunity for your child to use all three chords—C, G⁷, and G—the rest position, and the repeat sign.

Introducing the Page

1. Point out that in this song there are actually two different *verses*! The verse is the main part of a song, and often tells a story. When two or more sections of a song have essentially the same music but different lyrics, each of these sections is considered one verse. The first time through the song, we sing the top line of lyrics shown under the music. When we repeat and play it a second time, we sing the second line of lyrics.

2. Look the song over with your child, and have them say everything they observe about the music. Do they mention the repeat sign? The three different chords? The rest in measure 8? Make sure they have observed everything before continuing.

Practice Suggestions

1. Slowly and evenly point at each quarter-note slash and say the name of the chord, saying "rest" at the quarter rests.

2. Repeat this activity with your child.

3. As you slowly and evenly point at the quarter-note slashes and rests, say the lyrics to the song, demonstrating how the words fall against the beats, and keep a steady beat as you return to the beginning for the repeat.

4. Repeat this activity with your child.

5. As you tap the beats on your lap, speak the lyrics to the song in rhythm, saying the top line the first time through and the bottom line on the repeat.

6. Repeat this activity with your child.

7. Now, you sing the lyrics as your child strums the chords.

Subsequent Lessons

1. It's important for your child to develop the habit of looking over a piece of music before beginning to practice. What is the time signature? What chords are used? Are there rests? Is there a repeat sign? The more we know about a piece before we play, the easier and more fun it is to learn!

2. Together, play along with Track 18.

Notes:

Love Somebody

The Three-String D^7 Chord

So far, your child has learned three chords (C, G^7, and C) and used two fingers (1 and 3). Now, it's time to use three fingers to play a bluesy new chord: D^7.

Introducing the Page

Demonstrate the D^7 chord for your child.

1. Start with finger 1 positioned as if for a C chord, with finger 1 on the 2nd string at the 1st fret.

2. Keeping your left elbow still and, very slightly rotating your forearm counter clockwise so that your pinky moves a little farther from the fretboard, add finger 2 to the 3rd string directly next to the 2nd fret.

3. Add your 3rd finger to the 3rd string, also directly next to the 2nd fret. Make sure it is not bumping into the 2nd string. Use the very tip of the finger.

4. Making sure all three fingers are right next to their frets, strum the top three strings. All three strings should ring out clearly.

5. Together, listen to Track 19.

6. Repeat steps 1–4 with your child.

Practice Suggestions

1. Point at each quarter-note slash in "My Fourth Chord" as you slowly and evenly count aloud, saying "1 2 3 4 1 2 3 4."

2. Counting aloud, slowly strum "My Fourth Chord."

3. When strumming this song is comfortable and easy, try playing along with Track 20.

Subsequent Lessons

Because the D^7 chord requires the use of three fingers at once, it may feel more difficult than the first three chords covered in this book. Continue to remind your child not to squeeze too hard with any finger. Try the Butterfly Finger Exercise with all three fingers at once. Your child should just place them all in position for the chord without any pressure, and then strum, slowly adding pressure until all three strings ring clearly. Remember, this is the first time they are using finger 2, so be sensitive to potential discomfort and keep practice sessions short. It's important to avoid frustration. Take breaks and review past songs until they are comfortable with the D^7 chord and ready to move ahead.

Notes:

The Three-String D⁷ Chord

Use finger 1 to press the 2nd string at the 1st fret. Use fingers 2 and 3 to press the 3rd and 1st strings at the 2nd fret.

Strum strings 3–2–1.

D⁷

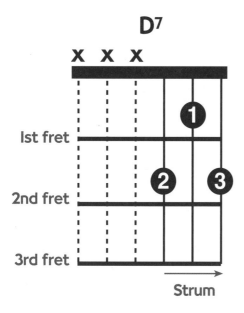

My Fourth Chord

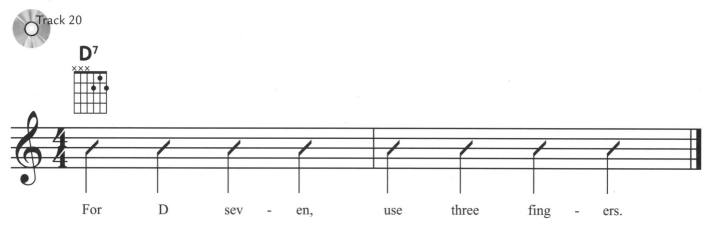

For   D   sev - en,   use   three   fing - ers.

Using D⁷ with Other Chords

This page gives your child the opportunity become accustomed to switching between D⁷ and the other chords. There are three exercises, and together they cover the following chord changes: G to D⁷, D⁷ to G, C to D⁷, D⁷ to C, G to G⁷, and G⁷ to C. The secret to changing smoothly between chords is to observe the fingers they have in common and plan the most efficient finger movement between them. Now would be a great time to start singing "When the Saints Go Marching In" and "Yankee Doodle" around the house!

Introducing the Page

Using the instructions below, demonstrate each chord change to your child, emphasizing the need for slow, direct finger movements. With a little planning, switching chords is easy! Show each chord individually, and then how to do each chord change called for in the three exercises. Allow them to master each chord change before playing the exercises.

Practice Suggestions

Exercise No. 1 covers the switches G to D⁷ and D⁷ to G. *Both chords use finger 3 on the 1st string.*

1. After strumming the G chord, release all pressure from finger 3, but *keep it in contact with the string.* Just lightly slide it from the 3rd fret down to the 2nd fret, as you place fingers 1 and 2 on their respective strings and frets for the D7 chord. Strum the top three strings.

2. After strumming the D⁷ chord, release all pressure from the fingers, but keep finger 3 in contact with the 1st string. Just lightly slide it from the 2nd fret up to the 3rd fret for the G chord. Strum.

Exercise No. 2 covers the switches of C to D⁷ and D⁷ to C. *Both chords use finger 1 on the 2nd string at the 1st fret.*

1. After strumming the C chord, keep light pressure on finger 1 as you slightly rotate the forearm counterclockwise and place fingers 2 and 3 on the 3rd and 1st strings, respectively, both directly next to the 2nd fret. Strum.

2. After strumming the D7 chord, release fingers 2 and 3 from their strings, and then slightly rotate the forearm clockwise, making sure your 1st finger is standing up on its tip so the 1st string can ring clearly as you strum the C chord.

Exercise No. 3 covers the switches C to D⁷, D⁷ to G, G to G⁷, and G⁷ to C. To review switching from C to D7, see the notes for Exercise No. 2, above. To review switching from D7 to G, see the notes for Exercise No. 1, above.

1. To switch from G to G7, simply release finger 3 from the 1st string at the 3rd fret as you place finger 1 on the same string at the 1st fret.

2. To switch from G7 to C, just release the pressure from the 1st finger on the 1st string and move it directly to the same fret on the 2nd string. Do this by lifting the finger just slightly—it should be a very small movement.

Using D⁷ with Other Chords

Practice Tip

Before you play "When the Saints Go Marching In" and "Yankee Doodle," practice the exercises on this page. They will help you to change chords easily.

Play each exercise very slowly at first, and gradually play them faster. Don't move on to the songs until you can easily move from chord to chord without missing a beat.

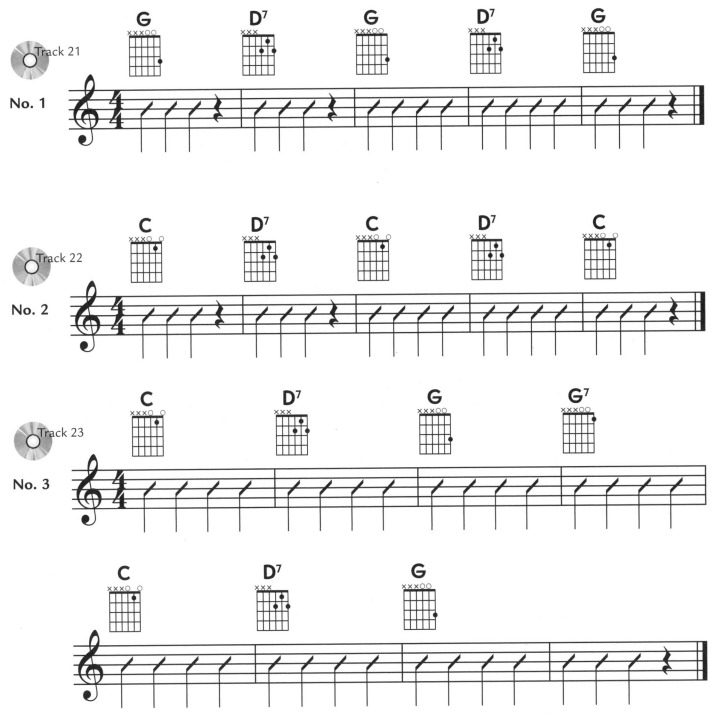

When the Saints Go Marching In

This song has a rest on the first beat. It features the chord changes G to D⁷, D⁷ to G, G to G⁷, G⁷ to C, and C to G.

Introducing the Page

If you spent adequate time mastering Exercises No. 1, 2, and 3 on page 41, your child will enjoy playing this fun song with little effort. Just remind them about the need for small, direct movements of the fingers and not to over-squeeze the strings. Encourage a light touch at all times.

It might be fun to talk about the song's roots in American gospel music, and its association with Dixieland jazz and the city of New Orleans.

Practice Suggestions

1. Try each chord change before beginning to play the song in rhythm. Make sure each change is clear in your child's mind and thus securely "under the fingers."

2. Count off one full measure before playing, making sure the student is ready to begin playing on the second beat instead of the first.

3. Tap out the beat on your lap as you sing and your child strums.

4. When the student is ready, try playing along with Track 24.

Subsequent Lessons

It will be fun for your child to try singing while he or she plays. Singing requires that they be very secure with playing the chords, so it's a good idea to wait a couple of weeks, after the song has matured a bit. It's important to stay with a song for a little while, rather than putting it down as soon as it's learned. It is, however, a bit of a balancing act because the child can become discouraged if they don't feel like they're "moving on." You know your child better than anyone! Keep your finger on the pulse of their enthusiasm and keep it high!

Notes:

When the Saints Go Marching In

Track 24

G

(rest) Oh when the saints   go march-ing   in,

D⁷

— Oh when the saints — go — march - ing — in,

G   **G⁷**   **C**

— Oh how I want — to be — in that num - ber —

G   **D⁷**   **G**

—— When the saints — go — march - ing — in.

Yankee Doodle

Nowadays, this fun song is considered patriotic, but your child may enjoy knowing that, originally, "doodle" was a word used to describe a silly person. It wasn't very nice! The song features the chord changes G to D^7, D^7 to G, G to C, C to D7, and C to G.

Introducing the Page

As with "When the Saints," if your child is properly prepared, this will be a fun song to play.

1. Point out the change from D7 to G going from measure 2 to measure 3; there are only two strums and then the chord changes. This is a great example of how it helps to look closely at the music before playing. Practice measures 1–3 several times before playing the whole song.

2. Point out the four rests in this song. They don't happen at obvious, regular intervals, so make sure your child is aware of them.

Practice Suggestions

1. Try each chord change before beginning to play the song in rhythm. Make sure each change is clear in your child's mind and thus securely "under the fingers."

2. Tap out the beat on your lap as you sing and your child strums.

3. When the student is ready, try playing along with Track 25.

Subsequent Lessons

Always look for opportunities to turn potential tricky spots into exercises for your child to master before beginning to play a song. Taken out of context, these spots can be easier to learn, and this will take the stress out of overcoming challenges some songs may present. That's what we did with measures 1–3 of this song. Just like carefully looking over the music before beginning to play, this kind of preparation can make learning to play guitar easier for your child.

As your child's guitar teacher, it is always best to be prepared for the lessons. If you are new to the guitar too, be sure to become comfortable with the material yourself before introducing it to your child.

Notes:

Yankee Doodle

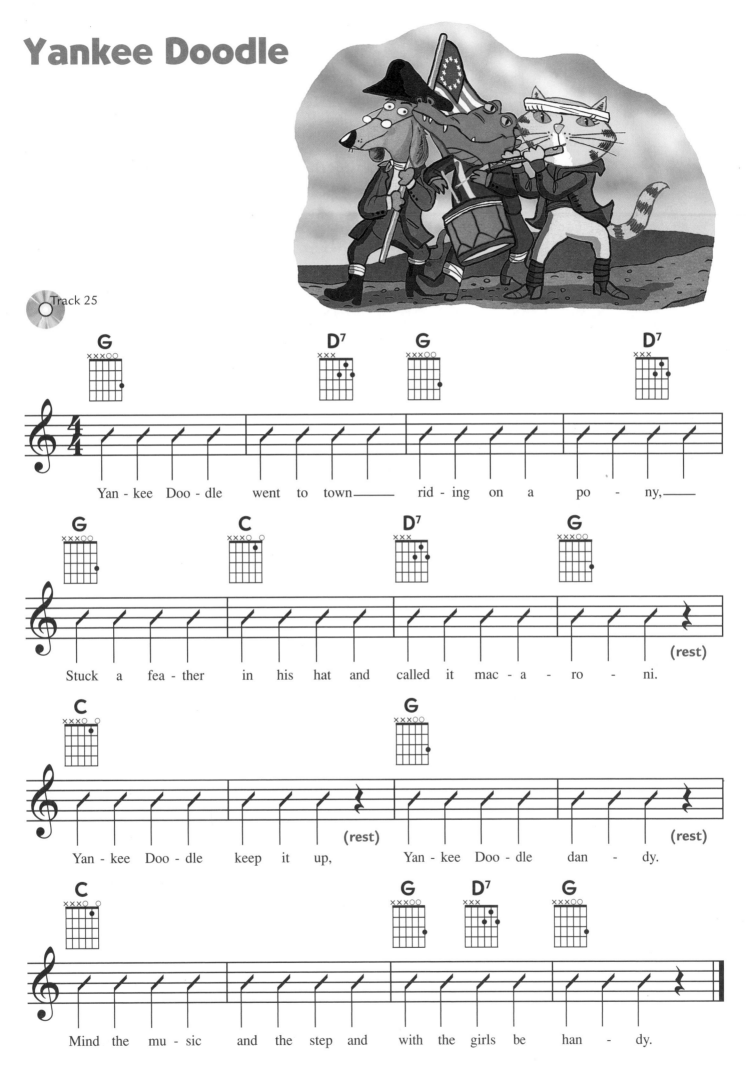

Track 25

| G | | D⁷ | G | | D⁷ |

Yan - kee Doo - dle   went to town—— rid - ing on a   po - ny,——

| G | C | D⁷ | G |

Stuck a fea - ther   in his hat and   called it mac - a - ro - ni.

(rest)

| C | G |

Yan - kee Doo - dle   keep it up,   Yan - kee Doo - dle   dan - dy.

(rest)   **(rest)**

| C | G | D⁷ | G |

Mind the mu - sic   and the step and   with the girls be   han - dy.

45

Getting Acquainted with Music Notation

Learning to read music notation will enable your child to read and play melodies on the guitar. This is a skill they will be able to use the rest of their life.

Introducing the Page

Review the material on page 47 with your child. Make sure he or she understand that:

1. Musical sounds are represented by *notes*.

2. Each kind of note looks different (discuss black notes, white notes, stems, and flags), and each lasts a different amount of time.

3. The time a note lasts is called its *note value*.

4. Notes and rests are written on a *staff*, the lines and spaces of which are numbered from the bottom up.

5. Where a note appears on a staff determines its note name.

6. Note names come from the musical alphabet, which is easy to learn because it has only seven letters: A B C D E F G.

7. Guitar music uses a *G clef*, often called the *treble clef*.

Practice Suggestions

For a few moments, skip ahead in the book to "Mary Had a Little Lamb" on page 81. Together, observe:

1. The combination of black notes and white notes.

2. Some notes are on lines, some are in spaces.

3. There are some chord strums mixed in with the melody notes.

Subsequent Lessons

As you move forward in the book, new notes and different time values will be introduced. Music is both an aural and a written language, and kids are *great* at learning new languages! The younger your child is, the more natural it is for them to learn a language, but try to be sensitive to the pace of learning. Make sure the student is *really reading the music* and *not* playing strictly by ear. Being able to play by ear is a true gift, but it should never get in the way of becoming a literate musician.

Notes:

Getting Acquainted with Music Notation

Notes

Musical sounds are represented by symbols called *notes*. Their time value is determined by their color (black or white), and by stems and flags attached to them.

The Staff

Each note has a name. That name depends on where the note is found on the *staff*. The staff is made up of five horizontal lines and the spaces between those lines.

5th LINE	4th SPACE
4th LINE	3rd SPACE
3rd LINE	2nd SPACE
2nd LINE	1st SPACE
1st LINE	

The Music Alphabet

The notes are named after the first seven letters of the alphabet (A–G).

A   B   C   D   E   F   G

Clefs

As music notation progressed through history, the staff had from two to twenty lines, and symbols were invented that would always give you a reference point for all the other notes. These symbols were called *clefs*.

Music for the guitar is written in the G or *treble clef*. Originally, the Gothic letter G was used on a four-line staff to show the pitch G.

This developed into the modern clef:

G

Getting Acquainted with Music Notation

It's time to start learning the names of the notes on the lines and spaces. The quarter note, which equals one beat, is also introduced.

Introducing the Page

Review the information on page 49 with your child.

1. Using the phrase **E**very **G**ood **B**ird **D**oes **F**ly makes it easy to learn the names of the notes on the lines, because from the bottom line up, they are E G B D F.

2. It might be fun for your child to make up his or her own phrase for learning the names of the notes on the lines.

3. The notes in the spaces, from the bottom up, form the word FACE.

4. Discuss the parts of the quarter note with your child, pointing out that it has a *stem* and the *note head* is black.

5. The chart showing the notes on the lines and spaces demonstrates how the stem of a quarter note can go up on the right side of the note head or down on the left side of the note head.

Practice Suggestions

1. Spend a little time making sure your child has learned the names of the notes on the lines and spaces.

2. Flip ahead in the book to page 89, and see if your child can point to the notes in "Aura Lee" and say their names. Flip back to page 49 and review as often as necessary.

3. Count aloud slowly, saying "1 2 3 4 1 2 3 4," etc., and point at the notes as you tap out on your lap the rhythms in "Clap and Count out Loud."

4. Now, point at the notes as your child counts with you and claps the rhythms in "Clap and Count out Loud."

Subsequent Lessons

Counting and clapping the rhythm should become an integral part of learning every new piece. This should become a habit and an important part of every practice session for years to come.

Notes:

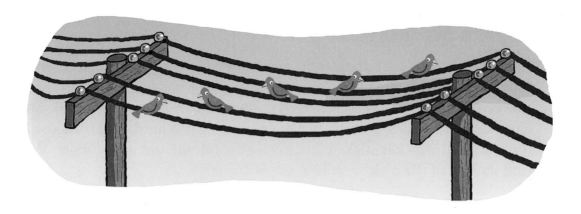

An easy way to remember the notes on the lines is using the phrase **E**very **G**ood **B**ird **D**oes **F**ly. Remembering the notes in the spaces is even easier because they spell the word **FACE**, which rhymes with "space."

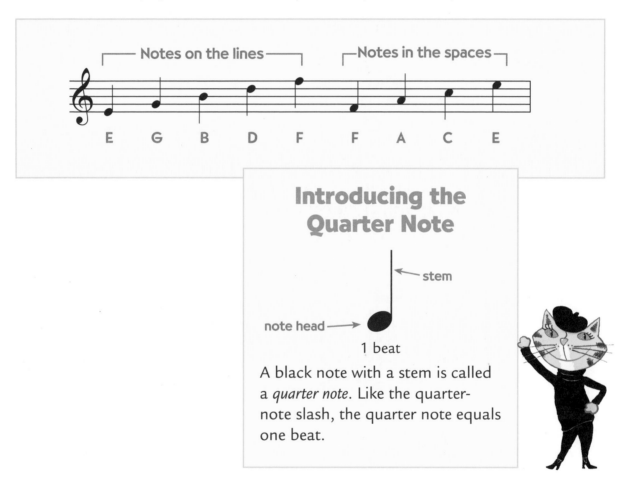

Introducing the Quarter Note

stem

note head →

1 beat

A black note with a stem is called a *quarter note*. Like the quarter-note slash, the quarter note equals one beat.

Track 26

Clap and Count out Loud

Notes on the First String: Introducing E

It's time for your child to become accustomed to picking a single string, as opposed to strumming three at once, as with the chords. This is an excellent time to review how to hold a pick, which is covered at the top of page 13. Make sure your child is holding it firmly but not squeezing too hard, and that just a small portion of the pick is sticking out below the thumb and index finger. We only use the very tip of the pick to strike a single string.

Introducing the Page

1. Review the information at the top of the page, pointing out that the names of the notes on the spaces spell the word "FACE" and the top space is called E.

2. Point out the circle (O) above the note head. This means to pluck the *open* string, which is a string that is not being fingered with the left hand.

3. Direct your child to the fretboard diagram at the top right of the page; point out how strings that are not being played are represented with dotted lines, and the string being played is a solid line.

4. Practice small *down strokes* (toward the floor) with the pick on the 1st string (the highest, thinnest string, closest to the floor).

5. Counting aloud slowly, demonstrate "Elizabeth the Elephant," the exercise using only E notes at the bottom of the page.

6. Have your child play along with you, as he or she counts aloud.

Practice Suggestions

1. It's always a good idea to count off one complete measure before you or your child begin to play. This sets the pace and lets them know when to begin playing. Explain that you'll say "1 2 3 4" and then he or she should start playing on the next "1." Demonstrate.

2. Just for fun, try saying the lyrics of the song, shown below the staff, in rhythm with your child while he or she plays.

Subsequent Lessons

Review good practice habits with your child often. They should remember to always look over the music carefully before they play, noting the time signature, saying the names of the notes, counting and clapping the rhythms, taking special note of rests, identifying any potential tricky spots, etc. The more thorough and careful the practice sessions, the quicker we learn to play and the more fun we have!

Notes:

Notes on the First String
Introducing E

A note sitting on the top space of the treble clef staff is called E. To play this note, pick the *open* 1st string (meaning without putting a left-hand finger on it).

Hear this note!

Track 27

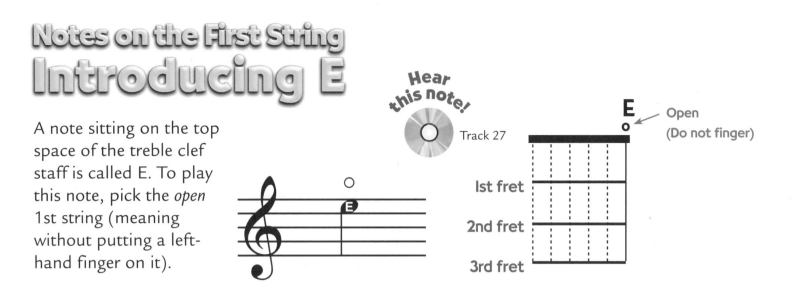

E
Open
(Do not finger)

1st fret
2nd fret
3rd fret

Elizabeth, the Elephant

Picking

- Play each E slowly and evenly, using a *downpick* motion. We will use only downpicks for the rest of the book.
- Use only a little motion to pick each note, just like strumming.

Track 28

Count: 1   2   3   4   1   2   3   4   1   2   3   4   1   2   3   4

El - e - phants eat   en - chil - a - das,   es - pe - cial - ly   E - li - za - beth.

The Note E with Chords

On this page, your child will learn to combine single notes and three-note-chord strums.

Introducing the Page

1. It's a good idea to discuss the subtle difference between picking a single string and strumming a three-string chord. Your child should use a small downward motion to pick the E note on the open E string, and only a slightly larger motion to strum the top three strings for the chord. Both motions are small and done mostly from the wrist.

2. Discuss the C and G7 chords, and how they are both played with finger 1 on the 1st fret. For the C chord, finger 1 is on the 2nd string; for the G7 chord, it's on the 1st string. Changing chords requires a very small movement.

Practice Suggestions

1. Practice "Note and Strum Warm-up." Notice the repeat sign and the rests on beat 4 of each measure.

2. Play it until both the picks and strums are played with ease, confidence, and accuracy.

3. Look over the music for "Note and Strum." Observe all the elements: the picks, the strums, the rests, the chord changes, etc.

4. Together, slowly point at each note and say, as appropriate, the name of the note or chord being picked or strummed, like this: "Pick E, strum C, strum C, rest," etc.

5. Counting slowly, demonstrate by playing the piece.

6. Now, count slowly and play through the song together.

7. Now, have your child play through the piece alone.

Subsequent Lessons

Strive to give your child more and more independence with their guitar playing. It's very helpful for you to demonstrate each new concept and skill, and to play along with him or her, but the more the student can play on their own, the better!

Notes:

The Note E with Chords

Practice Tip

For this tune, notice that both the C and G⁷ chords are fingered with finger 1 at the first fret.

C Chord

G⁷ Chord

Simply move your finger over one string to change chords.

Track 29

Note and Strum Warm-up
Before playing "Note and Strum" practice this exercise slowly until you are comfortable playing a note followed by a strum.

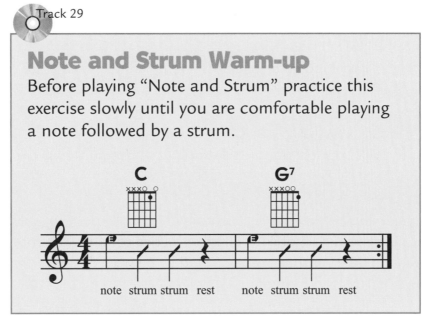

Note and Strum

Track 30

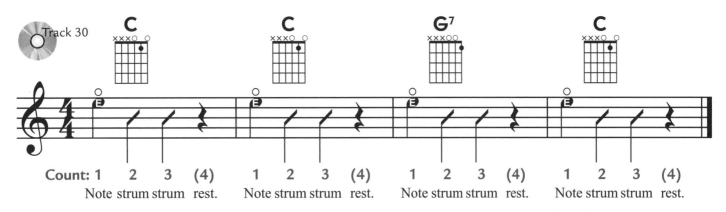

Notes on the First String: Introducing F

Remember "Every Good Bird Does Fly"? That's the phrase we used for memorizing the names of the notes on the staff, and "Fly" corresponds to the top line of the staff, so, a note placed on that line is called "F." You'll notice that playing an F note is a lot like playing a three-string G⁷ chord, because the F is the only fingered note in that chord.

Introducing the Page

1. Ask your child to play a three-string G⁷ chord.

2. Now, ask them to keep their left hand in that position and pick just the 1st string, like they did to play the E note. Congratulate your child for playing a new note!

3. Draw your child's attention to the picture of the F note on the staff, the fretboard diagram, and the photograph on page 55.

Practice Suggestions

1. Practicing "Up-Down-Up Warm-up" will prepare your child to play the song.

2. Point at each note of "Up-Down-Up" and say the name of the note aloud.

3. Repeat this activity with your child.

4. Point at each note and say the fingering aloud, saying "O" for "open" and "1" for the 1st finger (for example, the first two measures are "O O O O 1 1 1 1").

5. Counting aloud slowly, demonstrate the example.

6. Now, have your child play the example while you slowly count together.

Subsequent Lessons

When learning to play single-note melodies, make pointing at notes and saying the finger numbers a part of your child's practice routine. The more clearly they know beforehand how the music is supposed to be played, the easier it will be to learn.

Notes:

Notes on the First String
Introducing F

A note on the top line of the staff is called F. To play this note, use finger 1 to press the 1st string at the 1st fret. Use a down-pick motion to play only the 1st string.

Hear this note!
Track 31

F
First finger

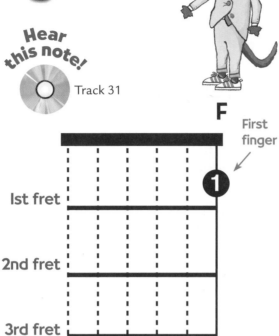

1st fret

2nd fret

3rd fret

Up-Down-Up

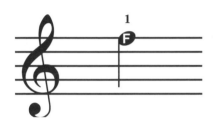

Track 32

Up-Down-Up Warm-up

Before playing "Up-Down-Up," practice this exercise until you are comfortable playing the note F.

Track 33

Start on E then up, first fin-ger. Down to E then up to the F.

The Notes E and F with Chords

This will be a fun and easy page because the left hand will be doing exactly what it did on page 53—moving finger 1 from the 1st fret, 2nd string to the 1st fret, 1st string.

Introducing the Page

1. Review the practice tip with your child. Point out that the only difference between the note F and the G^7 chord is how many strings are played with the pick. For the F, pick just the 1st string. For the G^7, strum the top three strings. The left-hand position is the same for both.

2. Carefully look over the music with your child. Observe which notes are picked and which are strummed. Picked single notes are written with round note heads; chord strums are written with strum slash marks.

3. As you did on page 53, together, slowly point at each note and say, as appropriate, the name of the note or chord being picked or strummed, like this: "Pick E, strum C, strum C, rest," etc.

4. Repeat this activity with your child.

5. Together, count aloud and clap the rhythm, saying "1 2 3 rest," etc.

Practice Suggestions

1. Slowly counting aloud, pick and strum through the music.

2. Have your child play along with you. Make sure he or she leaves finger 1 down when going from measure 2 to measure 3.

3. Let your child play through it alone.

Subsequent Lessons

1. Play the example as many as times as needed.

2. Play along with the recording.

Notes:

The Notes E and F with Chords

Practice Tip

For this tune, notice that the note F and the G⁷ chord are both fingered with finger 1 at the 1st fret on the 1st string.

Note F

G⁷ Chord

Don't lift your 1st finger between the note F and the G⁷ chord.

Track 34

Hold down 1st finger

E strum strum rest.   F strum strum rest.   One more time rest,   then you can rest.

Notes on the First String: Introducing G

The note G sits on the first space above the staff. It is played with finger 3 at the 3rd fret of the 1st string.

Introducing the Page

1. Ask your child to play a three-string G chord (review page 31, if necessary).

2. Now, ask him or her to keep their left hand in that position and pick just the 1st string, like they did to play the E and F notes. Congratulate your child for playing a new note!

3. Draw your child's attention to the picture of the G note on the staff, the fretboard diagram, and the photograph on page 59.

Practice Suggestions

1. Practicing "G Warm-up" will prepare your child to play "The Mountain Climber."

2. Point at each note of "The Mountain Climber" and say the name of the note aloud. For the chords, say "strum C" or "strum G," as appropriate.

3. Repeat this activity with your child.

4. Point at each note and say the fingering aloud, saying "O" for "open," "1" for the 1st finger, and "3" for the 3rd finger.

5. Counting aloud slowly, demonstrate the example.

6. Now, have your child play the example while you slowly count together.

Subsequent Lessons

The more notes and chords being used in a song, the more important it is for your child to have good practice habits. Make sure he or she always looks over the music, names the notes, names the fingers, counts and claps the rhythms, and plays slowly at first. Once your child can play a song exercise securely and confidently, let them play along with the recording.

Notes:

Notes on the First String
Introducing G

Hear this note!  Track 35

A note on the space above the staff is called G. Use finger 3 to press the 1st string at the 3rd fret. Use a downpick motion to play only the 1st string.

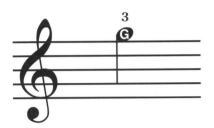

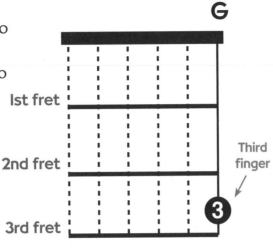

G

1st fret

2nd fret

Third finger

3rd fret

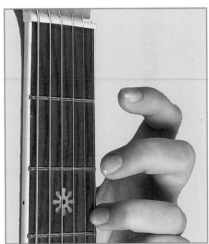

Track 36

G Warm-up

The Mountain Climber

Track 37

From the bot-tom to the top, the fear-less climb-er does not stop.

With his pick and tuned gui-tar, the pre-pared climb-er will go far.

The Notes E, F, and G with Chords

The note G and the G chord are both fingered with finger 3 at the 3rd fret on the 1st string.

Introducing the Page

1. Review the practice tip with your child and remind them to hold finger 3 on its note when switching from the G note to the G chord.

2. Carefully look over the music with your child. Observe which notes are picked and which are strummed. Picked single notes are written with round note heads; chord strums are written with strum slash marks.

3. As you did on page 53, together, slowly point at each note and say, as appropriate, the name of the note or chord being picked or strummed.

4. Repeat this activity with your child.

5. Point out that "Brave in the Cave" has only quarter notes and quarter-note slashes; there are no rests or longer notes.

Practice Suggestions

1. Slowly counting aloud, pick and strum through the music.

2. Make an exercise out of going from measure 3 into measure 4, and emphasize that the 3rd finger is held down when switching from the single note to the G chord.

3. Have your child play along with you. Make sure he or she leaves finger 3 down when going from measure 3 to measure 4.

4. Let your child play through it alone.

Subsequent Lessons

1. Play the example as many as times as needed.

2. Play along with the recording.

Notes:

The Notes E, F, and G with Chords

Practice Tip

Notice that the note G and the G chord are both fingered with finger 3 at the 3rd fret on the 1st string.

Note G

G Chord

Hold down the 3rd finger between the notes G and the G chord.

Brave in the Cave

Track 38

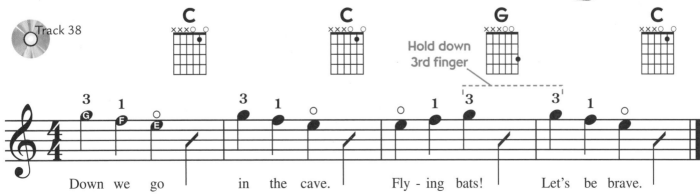

Hold down 3rd finger

Down we go   in the cave.   Fly - ing bats!   Let's be brave.

Single Notes, Then Chord! Chord! Chord!

This song uses all three of the single notes your child has used, plus the C and G⁷ chords.

Introducing the Page

1. "Note and Strum Warm-up" from page 53 is a good warm-up for this song.

2. Make measures 3 and 4 an exercise. Have your child play them over and over until those measures are easy for them to play.

Practice Suggestions

1. Point at the notes and say their names.

2. Point at the notes and say the fingerings.

3. Count aloud and clap the rhythms.

4. Demonstrate the song as your child counts aloud with you.

5. Have your child count and play with you.

6. Have your child count and play alone.

Subsequent Lessons

1. Continue practicing "Single Notes, Then Chord! Chord! Chord!" as needed.

2. Play along with the audio.

Notes:

Single Notes, Then Chord! Chord! Chord!

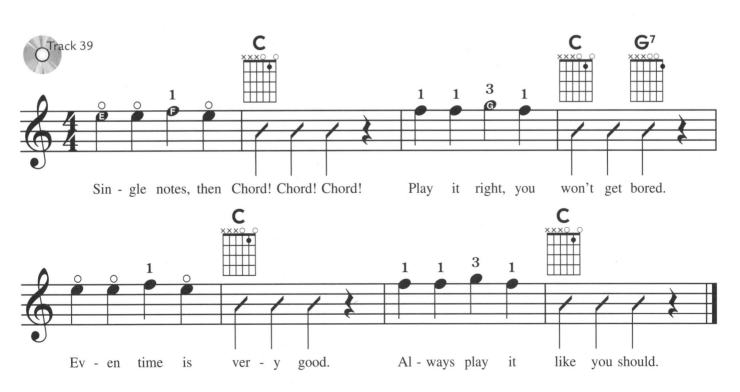

Track 39

Sin - gle notes, then Chord! Chord! Chord!   Play it right, you won't get bored.

Ev - en time is ver - y good.   Al - ways play it like you should.

Pumpkin Song

This song also uses all three of the single notes your child has used, plus the C and G⁷ chords.

Introducing the Page

1. "Note and Strum Warm-up" from page 53 is also a good warm-up for this song.

2. Point out to your child that measures 5 and 6 are exactly the same as measures 1 and 2.

Practice Suggestions

1. Point at the notes and say their names.

2. Point at the notes and say the fingerings.

3. Count aloud and clap the rhythms.

4. Demonstrate the song as your child counts aloud with you.

5. Have your child count and play with you.

6. Have your child count and play alone.

Subsequent Lessons

1. Continue practicing "Pumpkin Song" as needed.

2. Play along with the audio.

Notes:

Pumpkin Song

Track 40

G⁷   **C**

Can - dle in his head.   Doesn't need to be fed.

G⁷   **C**

Makes a tas - ty pie.   Seeds help witch - es fly!

Parent Guide

Notes on the Second String: Introducing B

A note on the middle line of the staff is called B, and it is played on the open 2nd string.

Introducing the Page

1. Since the 2nd string is an inside string (it's neither the closest to the ground nor the closest to the ceiling), playing it will take some getting used to. Until your child gets a "feel" for it, they may have to look at their right hand often, especially when the music calls for changing strings. Encourage them to keep their eyes on the music as soon as you can.

2. Draw your child's attention to the picture of the B note on the staff and the fretboard diagram on page 67.

3. "B Warm-up" will help your child prepare for "Two Open Strings" and "Two-String Melody." Note the repeat sign.

Practice Suggestions

For both songs:

1. Point at the notes and say their names.

2. Point at the notes and say the fingerings. Since there are two strings now, when naming the fingerings for the open strings, say "O 1st" or "O 2nd."

3. Demonstrate the song as your child counts aloud with you.

4. Have your child count and play with you.

5. Have your child count and play alone.

Subsequent Lessons

1. Continue practicing "Two Open Strings" and "Two-String Melody" as needed.

2. Play along with the recording.

Notes:

Notes on the Second String
Introducing B

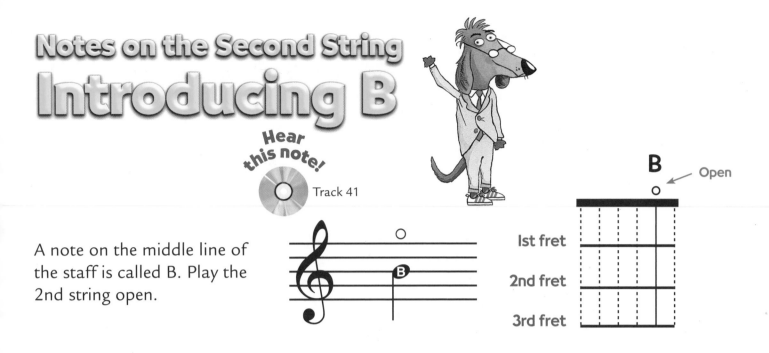

Hear this note!
Track 41

A note on the middle line of the staff is called B. Play the 2nd string open.

B — Open

1st fret
2nd fret
3rd fret

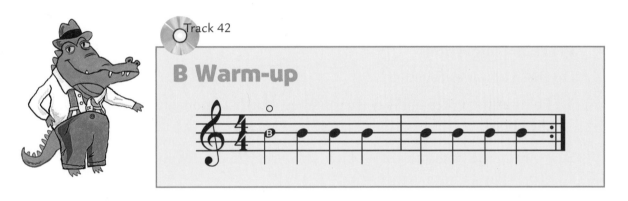

Track 42

B Warm-up

Two Open Strings

Track 43

Play the B string, now, the E string. B string, E string. Keeps you think-ing.

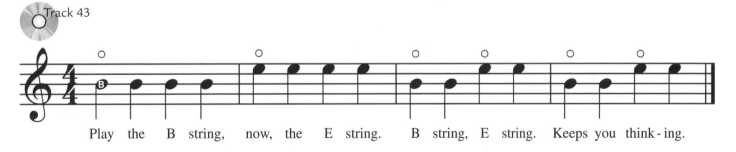

Two-String Melody

Track 44

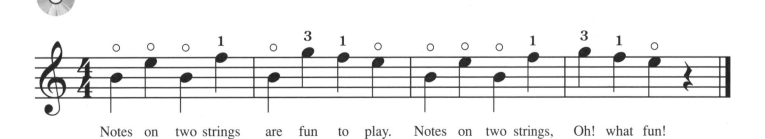

Notes on two strings are fun to play. Notes on two strings, Oh! what fun!

Jumping Around

"Jumping Around" features switching between the 1st and 2nd strings, and the fingers 1 and 3.

Introducing the Page

1. Review the G⁷ chord (page 23) and the G chord (page 31).

2. Without picking or strumming, put finger 1 in position for a G⁷ chord (finger 1 on the 1st string, 1st fret) then switch to putting finger 3 in position for a G chord (finger 3 on the 1st string, 3rd fret). Switch back and forth between the two positions.

3. Add strumming to step 2. Strum the top three strings.

4. Now, add picking the 1st string to step 2, instead of strumming.

5. Point out that measures 5 and 6 are exactly the same as measures 1 and 2.

Practice Suggestions

Do these activities together:

1. Point at the notes and say their names. If it is a chord, just say the name of the chord.

2. Point at the notes and say which string they're on, saying "2nd 1st 2nd 1st," etc. If it is a chord, say "strum."

3. Point at the notes and say the finger numbers: "O 1 O 3." If it is a chord, you can still say the finger numbers—measure 2 would be "1 3 1 rest."

4. Play measures 1 and 2 slowly until comfortable.

5. Play measures 2 and 3 slowly until comfortable.

6. Play measures 1, 2, and 3 slowly until comfortable.

7. Play measures 3 and 4 slowly until comfortable.

8. Play measures 1, 2, 3, and 4 slowly until comfortable.

9. Continue to work through the song in this manner.

Subsequent Lessons

The procedure described in steps 4–9 above is called *additive practice*. This is a great way to quickly master a new piece. Here is a slogan that you and your child should say together, often: SLOW AND STEADY WINS THE RACE.

Notes:

Jumping Around

Track 45

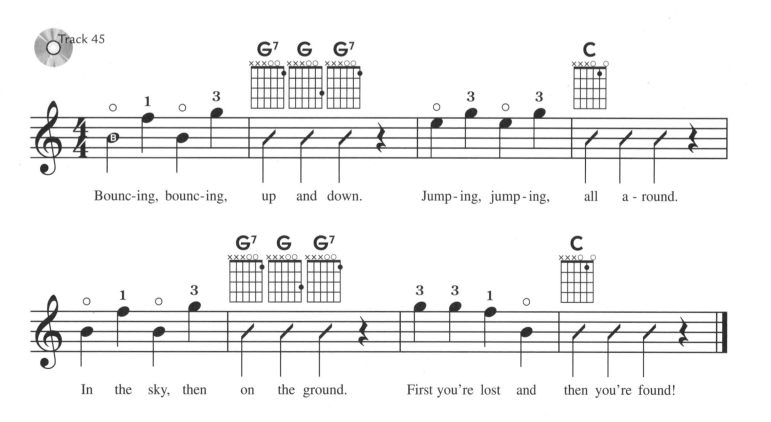

Bounc-ing, bounc-ing, up and down. Jump-ing, jump-ing, all a - round.

In the sky, then on the ground. First you're lost and then you're found!

Notes on the Second String: Introducing C

A note on the 3rd space of the staff is called C. Use finger 1 to press the 2nd string at the 1st fret. Pick only the 2nd string. This fingering is the same as for a three-string C chord.

Introducing the Page

1. Review the C chord (page 19).

2. Draw your child's attention to the picture of the C note on the staff, the fretboard diagram, and the photograph on page 71.

3. Have your child position the left hand as for a C chord, with finger 1 on the 2nd string at the 1st fret, then, instead of strumming, pick just the 2nd string.

4. Congratulate him or her for having learned a new note!

5. Practicing "C Warm-up" will prepare your child for "Ping Pong Song" and "Soccer Game."

6. Notice that in the last measure of "Soccer Game," the 1st finger holds down the C on the 2nd string as you pluck the open 1st string E note. This will require playing on the very tip of the finger, being careful not to interfere with the vibration of the 1string.

Practice Suggestions

Do these activities together for both songs:

1. Point at the notes and say their names.

2. Point at the notes and say which string they're on.

3. Point at the notes and say the finger numbers.

4. Use additive practice, mastering two measures at a time before adding them to measures previously mastered.

Subsequent Lessons

Practice both songs until secure, confident, and fluent enough to play along with the recording without error or confusion. Ease, accuracy, and confidence will never result from difficulty, error, and insecurity. SLOW AND STEADY WINS THE RACE.

Notes:

Notes on the Second String
Introducing C

Hear this note! Track 46

A note on the 3rd space of the staff is called C. Use finger 1 to press the 2nd string at the 1st fret. Pick only the 2nd string.

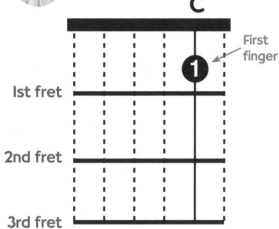

First finger

Track 47

C Warm-up

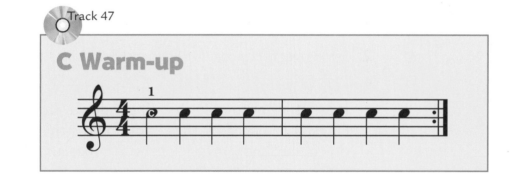

Ping Pong Song

Track 48

O - pen B string, first fin - ger C, down to B then up to C.

Soccer Game

Track 49

Hold

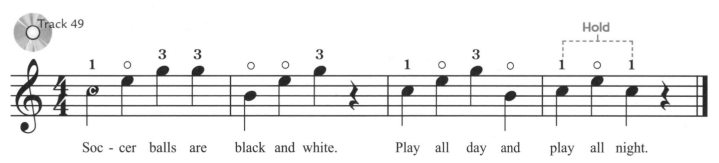

Soc - cer balls are black and white. Play all day and play all night.

71

The Half Rest

A *half rest* means do not play for two beats, which is the same as two consecutive quarter rests.

Introducing the Page

1. Draw your child's attention to the half rest on the staff in the yellow box on page 73.

2. Look over "Clap and Count out Loud" with your child and point out the two different kinds of rests used (half rests and quarter rests).

3. Count aloud as you clap the rhythms in the "Clap and Count out Loud" exercise. Spread your hands apart during the rests.

4. Do this together with your child.

When I Feel Best

This song uses lots of the notes your child knows, the D7 and G chords, and both the quarter and half rests.

Introducing the Page

1. Review the D7 chord with your child (page 39).

2. Look over the music for "When I Feel Best" together with your child.

3. Notice that finger 1 is used for both the C note and the D7 chord, so it is most efficient to hold that finger down when switching between the two. Finger 1 is placed on the C note on the third beat of the song and is held down until the last beat of the 5th measure, when it must be lifted to play the B note on the open 2nd string.

Practice Suggestions

Do these activities together with your child:

1. Point at the notes and say their names. Just say the names of the chords.

2. Point at the notes and say which string they're on. Just say "strum" for the chords.

3. Point at the notes and say the finger numbers. For the D7 chord, the fingers are 2-1-3.

4. Use additive practice, mastering two measures at a time before adding them to measures previously mastered.

Subsequent Lessons

Practice "When I Feel Best" for as many days as necessary, until it is smooth, secure, and confident. When your child can play along with Track 51 without error, it is mastered.

The Half Rest

Introducing the Half Rest

This rest means do not play for two beats, which is the same as  .

 Track 50

Clap and Count out Loud

$\frac{4}{4}$

1 2 3 4   1 2 (3) (4)   1 (2) 3 (4)   (1) (2) 3 4

(rest)(rest)   (rest) (rest)   (rest)(rest)

Practice Tip

Notice that the note C and the D⁷ chord are both fingered with finger 1 at the 1st fret on the 2nd string.

In "When I Feel Best," hold the 1st finger down from the third beat of the 1st measure until the last beat of the 5th measure.

Note C   **D⁷ Chord**

When I Feel Best

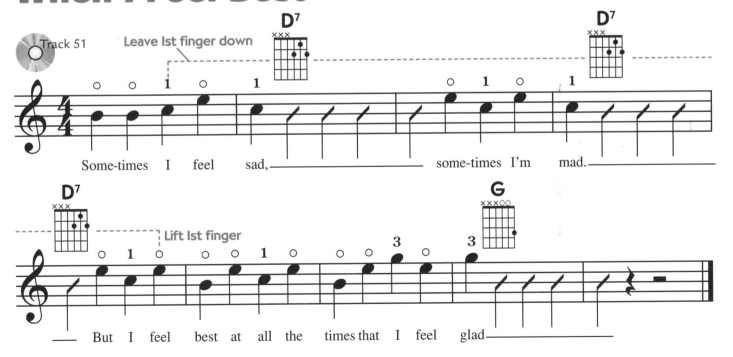

Notes on the Second String: Introducing D

A note on the 4th line of the staff is called D. The D note is played with the 3rd finger at the 3rd fret of the 2nd string.

Introducing the Page

1. Draw your child's attention to the picture of the D note on the staff, the fretboard diagram, and the photograph on page 75.

2. Practicing "D Warm-up" will prepare your child for "A-Choo!"

3. Count aloud as you clap the rhythms in "A-Choo!" Be sure to spread your hands apart during the rests.

4. Do this together with your child.

5. When possible, it is best to hold down finger 1 while playing finger 3. Make measure 3 an exercise: have your child play it over and over without lifting finger 1. Hold it down while playing the D note with finger 3. If your child's hand is too small or lacks the necessary reach to do this, it's okay. You can try this again after he or she has grown a little.

Practice Suggestions

Do these activities together with your child:

1. Point at the notes and say their names.

2. Point at the notes and say which string they're on.

3. Point at the notes and say the finger numbers.

4. Use additive practice, mastering two measures at a time before adding them to measures previously mastered.

Subsequent Lessons

Practice "A-Choo!" for as many days as necessary, until it is smooth, secure, and confident. When your child can play along with Track 54 without error, it is mastered. If it is possible for them, look for every opportunity to encourage your child to hold finger 1 down while playing finger 3.

Notes:

Notes on the Second String
Introducing D

Hear this note! Track 52

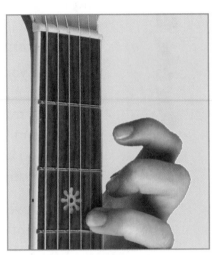

A note on the 4th line of the staff is called D. Use finger 3 to press the 2nd string at the 3rd fret. Pick only the 2nd string.

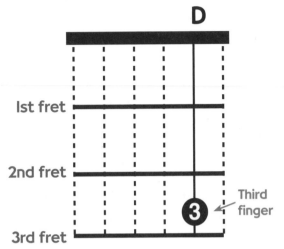

D

1st fret

2nd fret

3rd fret

Third finger

Track 53

D Warm-up

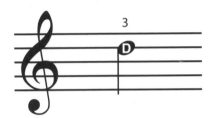

A-Choo!

Track 54

B and C and D are eas - y. Spil - ling pep - per makes me sneez - y.

"A - a - choo! A - a - choo!" Pep - per makes me go "A - choo!"

The Half Note

Like the half rest, the *half note* lasts two beats. It is twice as long as a quarter note. By the way, this would be a good time to start singing "Jingle Bells" around the house, even if it is not yet the holiday season. You'll be playing it soon.

Introducing the Page

1. Draw your child's attention to the picture of the half note on page 77. Point out that the note head is an open circle and that it has a stem. The stem can go up from the right side of the note head or down from the left side. The half notes in "Clap and Count out Loud" go up from the right, but in "Ode to Joy," they go down from the left. Generally, notes on the 3rd line or higher have down-stems and notes below that line have up-stems.

2. Look over "Clap and Count out Loud" with your child and point out the two different kinds of notes used (quarter notes and half notes). As you clap, hold your hands together for the two beats of each half note.

Practice Suggestions

Do these activities together with your child:
1. Point at the notes and say their names. Just say the names of the chords.

2. Point at the notes and say which string they're on.

3. Point at the notes and say the finger numbers.

4. Use additive practice, mastering two measures at a time before adding them to measures previously mastered.

Subsequent Lessons

Be sure to reinforce the fundamentals with your child: holding the guitar, how to hold the pick, and left-hand position and technique. Also, find a recording of Beethoven's *9th Symphony* and listen to it around the house. When the 4th Movement is playing, does your child recognize the "Ode to Joy" melody? Singing and listening to music are both part of learning to play. Keep your child engaged in music in as many ways as you can. It will provide entertainment for the whole family.

Notes:

The Half Note

Introducing the Half Note

2 beats

This note lasts two beats.
It is twice as long as a quarter note.

Track 55

Clap and Count out Loud

Ode to Joy
from Beethoven's 9th Symphony

Track 56

Ludwig van Beethoven

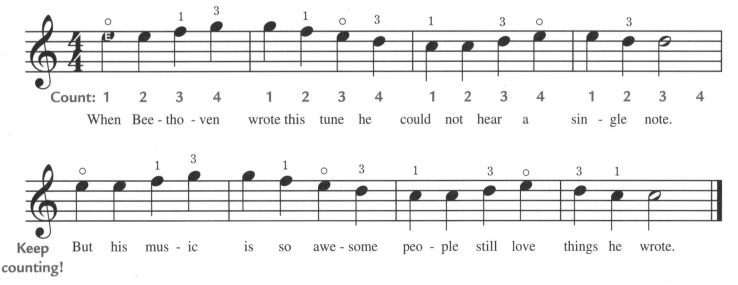

Count: 1 2 3 4   1 2 3 4   1 2 3 4   1 2 3 4

When Bee-tho-ven wrote this tune he could not hear a sin-gle note.

Keep counting!

But his mus-ic is so awe-some peo-ple still love things he wrote.

Jingle Bells

"Jingle Bells" features the three-string C and G chords, quarter rests, and notes on both the 1st and 2nd strings. This would be a good time to start singing "Mary Had a Little Lamb" around the house. It's the next song in this book.

Introducing the Page

1. Review the music with your child, pointing out the half notes, chord strums, and quarter rests. Quarter notes comprise the rest of the song.

2. Make the last two measures an exercise for your child to repeat. It combines the biggest challenges in this song: reaching from finger 3 to finger 1, switching from single notes to chord strums, and using the rest position to perform the quarter rest.

Practice Suggestions

Do these activities together with your child:

1. Point at the notes and say their names. Just say the names of the chords.

2. Point at the notes and say which string they're on.

3. Point at the notes and say the finger numbers.

4. Use additive practice, mastering two measures at a time before adding them to measures previously mastered.

5. Sing while you play. It's fun!

Subsequent Lessons

1. Review "Jingle Bells" as needed.

2. Play "Jingle Bells" with the recording.

Notes:

Jingle Bells

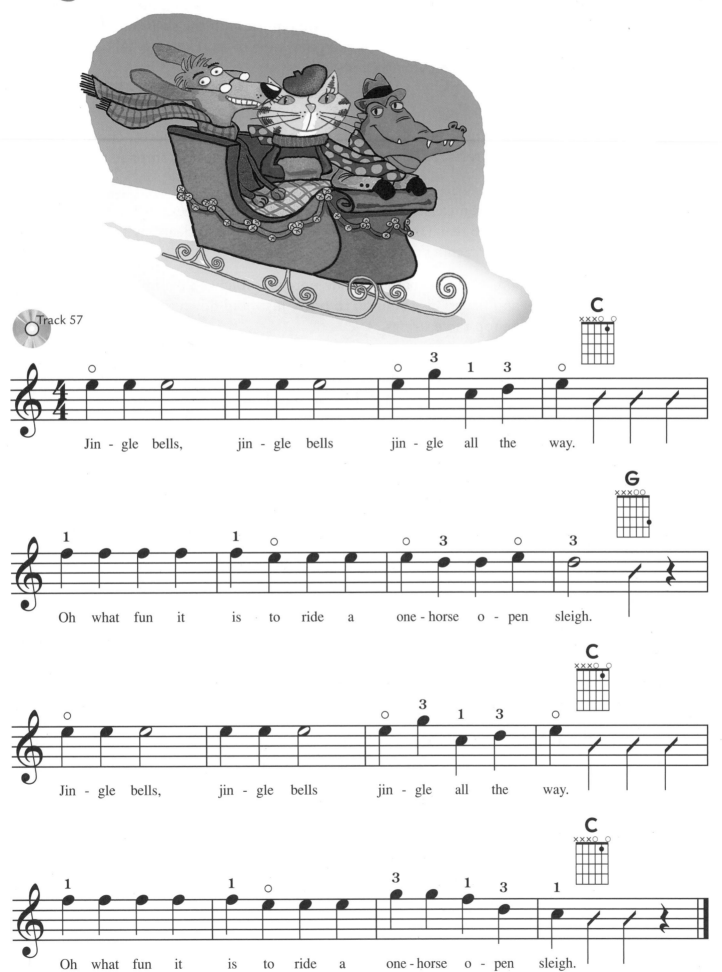

Track 57

C

Jin - gle bells, jin - gle bells jin - gle all the way.

G

Oh what fun it is to ride a one - horse o - pen sleigh.

C

Jin - gle bells, jin - gle bells jin - gle all the way.

C

Oh what fun it is to ride a one - horse o - pen sleigh.

Mary Had a Little Lamb

"Mary Had a Little Lamb" has all of the same notes, chords, and rests as "Jingle Bells." It is another chance to enjoy playing music with the skills and knowledge your child has learned so far. This is a good time to start singing "Allouette" around the house. It's coming up soon!

Introducing the Page

1. Review the music with your child, pointing out the half notes, chord strums, and quarter rests. As with "Jingle Bells," quarter notes comprise the rest of the song.

2. Make the first measure an exercise for your child to repeat. It's a great exercise for learning to reach from finger 3 to finger 1, and for learning to hold finger 1 down when reaching for finger 3.

3. In measure 4, notice that the single-note G is followed by the three-string G chord, and finger 3 is common to both. Just hold down finger 3 and then strum the top three strings.

4. Similarly, in measure 8, just hold down the single-note C and then strum the top three strings to play the C chord. Be sure not to let finger 1 interfere with the vibration of the open 1st string in the chord.

5. Line 3 is the same as line 1, and line 4 is the same as line 2.

Practice Suggestions

Do these activities together with your child:

1. Point at the notes and say their names. Just say the names of the chords.

2. Point at the notes and say which string they're on.

3. Point at the notes and say the finger numbers.

4. Use additive practice, mastering two measures at a time before adding them to measures previously mastered.

5. Sing while you play!

Subsequent Lessons

1. Review "Mary Had a Little Lamb" as needed.

2. Play "Mary Had a Little Lamb" with the recording.

Notes:

Mary Had a Little Lamb

Track 58

Mary had a little lamb, little lamb, little lamb,

Mary had a little lamb, its fleece was white as snow.

Ev - 'ry - where that Mary went, Mary went, Mary went,

Ev - 'ry - where that Mary went, the lamb was sure to go.

Notes on the Third String: Introducing G

A note on the 2nd line of the staff is called G, and it is played by picking the open 3rd string.

Introducing the Page

1. Draw your child's attention to the picture of the G note on the staff, the fretboard diagram, and the photograph on page 83.

2. Practicing "G Warm-up" will prepare your child for "Three Open Strings" and "Little Steps and Big Leaps."

3. Learn "Three Open Strings" first, and make sure your child is comfortable moving the pick from string to string.

4. Count aloud as you clap the rhythms in "Little Steps and Big Leaps." Be sure to spread your hands apart during the rests.

5. Do this together with your child.

6. As always, it is best to hold a finger on a note that will be played again very soon. For example, the D note in measure 1, beat 3 is played again in measure 2, beat 1, so it is best to keep finger 3 on or near the 2nd string at the 3rd fret while playing the E note on measure 1, beat 4.

7. Make measure 6 an exercise to repeat many times. In this measure, we play the high G note on the 1st string, then skip down to the low G note on the 3rd string. The distance from the high G to the low G is called an *octave* (the closest distance between two notes with the same name).

Practice Suggestions

Do these activities together with your child:

1. Point at the notes and say their names.

2. Point at the notes and say which string they're on.

3. Point at the notes and say the finger numbers, saying "O" for open strings.

4. Use additive practice, mastering two measures at a time before adding them to measures previously mastered.

Subsequent Lessons

Practice "Little Steps and Big Leaps" for as many days as necessary, until it is smooth, secure, and confident. When your child can play along with Track 62 without error, it is mastered. Encourage your child to learn to skip from string to string with the pick without looking at the right hand.

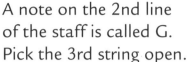
Notes on the Third String
Introducing G

Hear this note!

Track 59

A note on the 2nd line
of the staff is called G.
Pick the 3rd string open.

Open

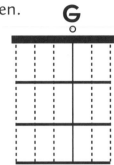

Track 60

G Warm-up

Three Open Strings

Track 61

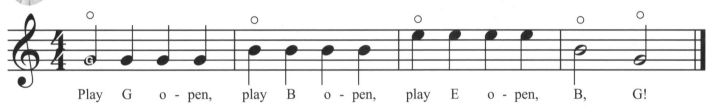

Play G o - pen, play B o - pen, play E o - pen, B, G!

Little Steps and Big Leaps

Track 62

Play - ing on three strings lets me play notes far a - part.

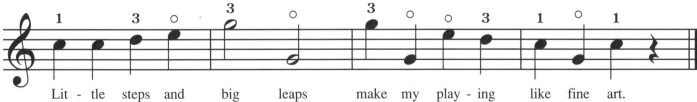

Lit - tle steps and big leaps make my play - ing like fine art.

Alouette

The first thing you'll notice about "Alouette" is that it's 24 measures long! It's easy to learn, though, because there is a lot of repetition. This French folk song is about a bird called a skylark, and plucking the feathers before cooking it for dinner. The words are translated as: "Little skylark, lovely little skylark, little lark, I'll pluck your feathers off."

Introducing the Page

1. The last eight measures are exactly the same as the first eight measures. Within those eight measures, measures 5, 6, and 7 are the same as measures 1, 2, and 3. Likewise, measures 21, 22, and 23 are the same as measures 17, 18, and 19.

2. Think of "Alouette" as having three sections: The "A" section is measures 1—8; the "B" section measures 9–16; and then the "A" section returns in measures 17–24. This is an A-B-A form. The words of the song (the *lyrics*) make this form easy to detect.

3. This song combines a single-note melody with strummed three-note chords. Notice, however, that every time you strum a chord, the single note just before it is part of the chord. Just leave the finger down and strum. Easy!

4. Count aloud as you clap the rhythms in "Alouette." Be sure to spread your hands apart during the rests.

5. Do this together with your child.

6. Make measures 15 and 16 an exercise to repeat many times; they include lots of string skipping with the pick. See if your child can learn to play these measures without looking at the right hand. It's okay, though, if they needs to sneak a peek every now and then. Switching attention from one hand to another and from the hands to the written music is a good skill for your child to develop.

Practice Suggestions

Do these activities together with your child:

1. Point at the notes and say their names.

2. Point at the notes and say which string they're on.

3. Point at the notes and say the finger numbers, saying "O" for open strings. Say "O-1-O" for the C chord and "O-O-3" for the G chord.

4. Use additive practice, mastering two measures at a time before adding them to measures previously mastered.

Subsequent Lessons

Practice "Alouette" for as many days as necessary, until it is smooth, secure, and confident. Sing the song together as your child plays. When your child can play along with Track 63 without error, it is mastered.

Alouette

A - lou - et - te, gen - tille A - lou - et - te,

A - lou - et - te, je te plu - mer - ai.

Je te plu - mer - ai la tête, Je te plu - mer - ai la tête.

Et la tête, et la tête, Ah! _____

A - lou - et - te, gen - tille A - lou - et - te,

A - lou - et - te, je te plu - mer - ai.

Notes on the Third String: Introducing A and the Whole Note

A note on the 2nd space of the staff is called A. To play an A, use finger 2 to press the 3rd string at the 2nd fret. Pick only the 3rd string. The whole note is an open circle with no stem, and it lasts four beats. Review the D⁷ chord on page 39 before starting this page.

Introducing the Page

1. Draw your child's attention to the picture of the A note on the staff, the fretboard diagram, and the photograph on page 87.

2. Practicing "A Warm-up" will prepare your child for "A Is Easy" and "Taking a Walk."

3. Together, look through "Clap and Count out Loud" and "A Is Easy," looking for the whole notes. Can your child find them?

4. Practice "Clap and Count out Loud," together.

5. Make measure 3 of "A Is Easy" an exercise for your child to repeat many times. It includes switching from finger 1 to finger 2 and from the 2nd string to the 3rd string.

6. Master "A Is Easy" before moving on to "Taking a Walk."

7. Count aloud as you clap the rhythms in "Taking a Walk." Be sure to take your hands apart during the rests.

8. Make measures 5 and 6 of "Taking a Walk" an exercise for your child to repeat. In measure 6, we switch from playing single notes to the D⁷ chord. In measure 5, keep finger 2 down on the A and finger 1 down on the C. You'll be more prepared for the D⁷ chord in measure 6. Just move finger 3 from the 2nd string, 3rd fret to the 1st string, 2nd fret, and *voila*! D⁷!

Practice Suggestions

Do these activities together with your child:
1. Point at the notes and say their names.

2. Point at the notes and say which string they're on.

3. Point at the notes and say the finger numbers: "2-1-3" for the D7 chord and "O-O-3" for the G chord.

4. Use additive practice, mastering two measures at a time before adding them to measures previously mastered.

Subsequent Lessons

Practice "Taking a Walk" for as many days as necessary, until it is smooth, secure, and confident. When your child can play along with Track 68 without error and without looking at the right hand, it is mastered.

Notes on the Third String
Introducing A

Hear this note!
Track 64

A note on the 2nd space of the staff is called A. Use finger 2 to press the 3rd string at the 2nd fret. Pick only the third string.

A

Second finger

Track 65

A Warm-up

Introducing the Whole Note

This note lasts four beats. It is as long as two half notes, or four quarter notes.

o

4 beats

Clap and Count out Loud

Track 66

1 2 3 4   1 2 3 4   1 2 3 4   1 2 3 4

A Is Easy!
Track 67

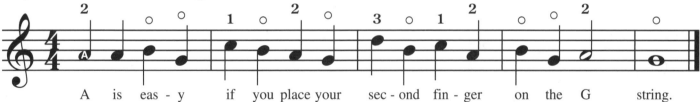

A is eas - y if you place your sec - ond fin - ger on the G string.

Taking a Walk
Track 68

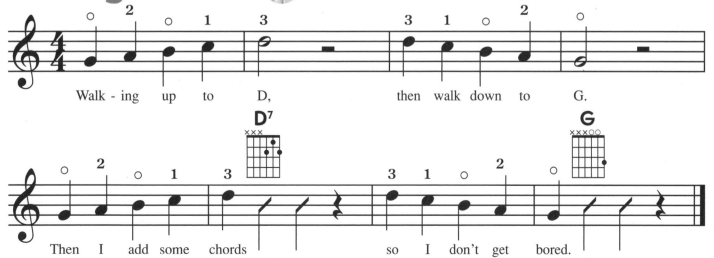

Walk - ing up to D, then walk down to G.

D⁷   **G**

Then I add some chords so I don't get bored.

87

Aura Lee

Does your child know who Elvis Presley was? An Internet search of his name, or even "Love Me Tender"—a song with the same melody as "Aura Lee"—may reward you and your child with photos, music, and videos to enjoy together.

Introducing the Page

1. Notice that there are two lines of lyrics under the music for measures 1–4. These are two verses of the song. The words "Aura Lee! Aura Lee!" are the *refrain*, or *chorus*. A refrain always pairs the same words with the same melody and is repeated often. Many songs have two verses before the refrain, as does this arrangement of "Aura Lee."

2. Notice the repeat sign at the end of measure 4.

3. This song uses quarter notes, half notes, and whole notes. Together with your child, look through the music and find the half notes, then find the whole notes.

4. Slowly counting aloud, clap the rhythms for the song. Hold your hands together during the half notes and whole notes.

Practice Suggestions

Do these activities together with your child:

1. Point at the notes and say their names.

2. Point at the notes and say which string they're on.

3. Point at the notes and say the finger numbers.

4. Use additive practice, mastering two measures at a time before adding them to measures previously mastered.

Subsequent Lessons

Practice "Aura Lee" for as many days as necessary, until it is smooth, secure, and confident. Sing the song together as your child plays. When your child can play along with Track 69 without error, it is mastered.

Notes:

Aura Lee

Track 69

Elvis Presley recorded this folk song as a pop ballad called "Love Me Tender."

1. As the black - bird in the spring · 'neath the wil - low tree,
2. sat and piped I heard him sing, sing of Au - ra Lee!

Au - ra Lee! Au - ra Lee! Maid of gold - en hair,

Sun - shine came a - long with thee and swal - lows in the air.

She'll Be Comin' 'Round the Mountain

This song combines all the single notes you know on the 1st, 2nd, and 3rd strings, strumming the G⁷ and C chords, and rests.

Introducing the Page

1. Look over the music together with your child and locate all of the rests. Remember to use the rest position to silence the strings for these rests.

2. Now look through the music again, and point out all of the chord strums.

3. Count aloud as you clap the rhythms in "She'll Be Comin' 'Round the Mountain." Be sure to spread your hands apart during the rests.

4. Do this together with your child.

Practice Suggestions

Do these activities together with your child:

1. Point at the notes and say their names.

2. Point at the notes and say which string they're on.

3. Point at the notes and say the finger numbers: "O" for open strings, "O-1-O" for the C chord, and "O-O-1" for the G⁷ chord.

4. Use additive practice, mastering two measures at a time before adding them to measures previously mastered.

Subsequent Lessons

Practice "She'll Be Comin' 'Round the Mountain" for as many days as necessary, until it is smooth, secure, and confident. Sing the song together as your child plays. When your child can play along with Track 70 without error, it is mastered.

Notes:

She'll Be Comin' 'Round the Mountain

Track 70

She'll be com - in' 'round the moun - tain when she comes. She'll be

com - in' 'round the moun - tain when she comes. She'll be

com - in' 'round the moun - tain, she'll be com - in' 'round the moun - tain, she'll be

com - in' 'round the moun - tain when she comes!

Review: Music Matching Games

Complete page 93 with your child one section at a time. Check the answers using the Answer Key.

Symbols

Notes and Strums:

Rests:

Time Signatures:

$\frac{4}{4}$ $\frac{3}{4}$

Chords:

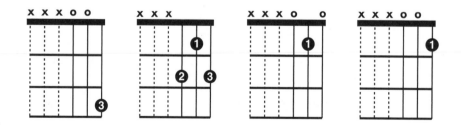

Repeat Sign:

G Clef:

Review: Music Matching Games

Chords

Draw a line to match each chord frame on the left to the correct photo on the right.

1.

2.

3.

4.

Symbols

Draw a line to match each symbol on the left to its name on the right.

1. o   Treble clef

2.   Quarter note

3.   Whole note

4.   Quarter slash

5.   Half note

6.   Double bar line

7.   Half rest

8.   Repeat sign

9.   Quarter rest

Notes

Draw a line to match each note on the left to its correct music notation on the right.

1. F

2. E

3. C

4. B

5. A

6. D

7. G

8. G

Answer Key

Chords
1: page 16; 2: page 20; 3: page 25; 4: page 31

Symbols
1: page 70; 2: page 63; 3: page 39; 4: page 10;
5: page 39; 6: page 28; 7: page 57; 8: page 18;
9: page 10

Notes
1: page 41; 2: page 46; 3: page 47; 4: page 52;
5: page 55; 6: page 59; 7: page 67; 8: page 70

93

Certificate of Completion

Complete the certificate on the next page and congratulate your child. This is an important achievement, so make sure to celebrate with a treat! Put this certificate on the wall above your lesson area or in a prominent place.